WHAT'S GOING TO HAPPEN?

Answering Your Prophetic Questions

WHAT'S GOING TO HAPPEN?

Answering Your Prophetic Questions

CARL G. JOHNSON

REGULAR BAPTIST PRESS
1300 North Meacham Road
Schaumburg, Illinois 60173-4888

Library of Congress Cataloging-in-Publication Data

Johnson, Carl G.
    What's going to happen? : answering your prophetic questions/
Carl G. Johnson.
        p. cm.
    Includes bibliographical references and index.
    ISBN 0-87227-173-0
    1. Bible—Prophecies—Miscellanea. 2. Eschatology—Miscellanea.
I. Title. II. Title: What's going to happen?
BS647.2.J645 1992
236—dc20   92-6597
                                                              CIP

WHAT'S GOING TO HAPPEN?
© 1992
Regular Baptist Press
Schaumburg, Illinois

Second printing—1993

Contents

Preface

Only three time periods exist for any man or for any nation—the past, the present and the future. We know the past, in part at least; but on the whole, we do not know the future. Nevertheless, both the past and the future exercise enormous influence over the present.

The future contains factors of fear for many people, especially because frightful catastrophes are now possible.

Dr. M. R. DeHaan wrote some time ago: "Not one in a hundred of the members of our evangelical churches could give the order of events of the last days, and hence do not know what to look for."[1]

In my evangelistic meetings through the years I have received written questions from hundreds of people concerning prophecy, or things that will happen in the future. The year in which I wrote this book was one of my busiest years in evangelism. Pastors and churches asked me to speak on prophecy more times that year than in any other year of my twenty-eight years in evangelism. People are vitally interested in the future now as never before. The message concerning the future is "being sounded from the pulpits and airwaves of mainstream Christian evangelists and resonantly striking a chord among tens of millions of conservative Christians. . . . Those who embrace dispensationalism find 'end is near' forecasts a powerful motivation for converting others to Christianity."[2]

I have collected these questions and stored them in my files for years. About a year ago I took them out, reread them and decided to try to answer them in print. I have had an extremely enjoyable and profitable time studying God's Word for answers to these questions about the future. I have written fourteen other books, but I can truthfully say this has been the one I have delighted to write more than any of the others. I have spent literally hundreds of hours in research and study, and I thank God for the things I have learned.

The Word of God from beginning to end is a great unfolding of the future, and the Holy Spirit has come to show us "things to come" (John 16:13). "I am God, and there is none else; I am God, and there is none like me, declaring the end from the beginning . . ." (Isa. 46:9, 10). A note in the Pilgrim Bible at verse 10 says: "Prophecy is simply prewritten history. God, Who is all wise, knows the future as well as the past. He has revealed much of that future through the predictive portions of the Bible. Some prophecies have been fulfilled, while others await fulfillment, but all of them must eventually be brought to pass."[3]

My prayer for every reader of this book is that you will be ready for the future and not afraid of it. Make sure you have trusted Jesus Christ as your personal Savior. As we think of the any-moment return of the Lord Jesus Christ, may each of us

look for Him (Phil. 3:20);

live for Him (2 Pet. 3:11, 14);

labor for Him (Luke 19:12, 13).

I am grateful for all the help I have received through the writings of others, and I pray that you will be helped by the answers I have given.

Acknowledgments

The author and publisher would like to acknowledge material

Reprinted by permission from *Confident Living,* Copyright © 1989 by the Good News Broadcasting Association, Inc.

Taken from: *The Future Life* by René Pache. Copyright 1962. Moody Bible Institute of Chicago. Moody Press. Used by permission.

Taken from: *The Revelation of Jesus Christ* by John F. Walvoord. Copyright 1966. Moody Bible Institute of Chicago. Moody Press. Used by permission.

Taken from: *The Wycliffe Bible Commentary.* Copyright 1962. Moody Bible Institute of Chicago. Moody Press. Used by permission.

Reprinted from WHY ME, LORD? by Paul W. Powell, published by Victor Books, 1981, SP Publications, Inc., Wheaton, IL 60187.

From: *The Revelation Record*
By: Henry M. Morris, © 1983
Used by permission of Tyndale House Publishers, Inc.

From: *The King Is Coming*
By: H. L. Willmington
© 1973, 1981, 1991 by Tyndale House Publishers, Inc.
All rights reserved.

Taken from the book PROFILES IN PROPHECY by S. Franklin Logsdon. Copyright © 1968 by Zondervan Publishing House. Used by permission.

Taken from the book THINGS TO COME by J. Dwight Pentecost. Copyright © 1958, 1964 by the Dunham Publishing Company. Used by permission of Zondervan Publishing House.

Q 1. After the Rapture, will any Christians be left here for the Tribulation? If not, who does Revelation 13:7 refer to as saints?

A Revelation 13:7 says, "And it was given unto him to make war with the saints, and to overcome them: and power was given him over all kindreds, and tongues, and nations." The context of this verse indicates it will take place during the middle of the tribulation period and that the Beast (Antichrist) will have power over the earth for the last forty-two months of that period. He will make war against the saints of God and will overcome them.

This verse does not refer to the believers of this present Church Age. The saints of this present age will be raptured before the tribulation period (1 Thess. 4:13–18). "Saints" refers to those whom God has saved and separated unto Himself. There were saints in the time of the Old Testament, before the Church Age, and saints during the time of the New Testament. There will be saints (saved ones) in the coming tribulation period. The saints of Revelation 13:7 will be those saved during the Tribulation, after the rapture of the Church.

The Devil will give the Beast power (Rev. 13:2, 4, 5, 7), his seat— a throne (v. 2), great authority (v. 2), a mouth (v. 5), occasion to make war with the saints (v. 7; cf. Dan. 7:21, 25) and ability to overcome them (v. 7). During the last half of the Tribulation, the Beast will seek to destroy everyone who worships the true God, and only those who have gone into hiding will escape death.

John Phillips, in his interesting book, *Exploring Revelation,* wrote concerning the Beast: "To war he goes with the refurbished equipment of the inquisition, with the rack, the thumbscrew, the stake, the boiling oil. To war he goes with his firing squads, gas chambers, long-prepared concentration camps, death pits."[4]

Q 2. What Scriptures show that the Second Coming has two phases: when Christ comes *for* His own and when He comes *with* His own?

A Many people believe in only one aspect, Christ's coming to the earth. However, the Bible distinguishes between the Rapture and the Second Coming and a period of approximately seven years between the two.

15

At the Rapture	At the Second Coming (Revelation)
Christ will come *for* His own (John 14:3).	Christ will come *with* His own (1 Thess. 3:13; Jude 14).
Only His own will see Him (1 Thess. 4:13–18).	Every eye will see Him (Rev. 1:7).
He will come in the air (1 Thess. 4:17).	He will come to the earth (Zech. 14:4; Acts 1:11, 12).
Living saints will be translated (1 Thess. 4:17).	No saints will be translated.
The saved ones will go to Heaven (1 Thess. 4:17).	The unsaved will remain on the earth. Satan will be bound and cast into the bottomless pit (Rev. 20:1, 2).
Satan will not be bound.	Satan will be bound and cast into the bottomless pit (Rev. 20:1, 2).
The world will continue in sin.	Christ will judge the world for sin (Isa. 13:9–11; 2 Thess. 1:7–9).
Christ will come *for* His Bride (John 14:3; 1 Thess. 4:16, 17; Rev. 19:7).	He will come *with* His Bride (Rev. 19:7–14).
Christ will come as the bright and morning star (Rev. 22:16).	Christ will come as the Sun of Righteousness (Mal. 4:2).
The Rapture has no signs preceding it.	Definite signs will precede the Second Coming (Luke 21:11, 25).
Christians will be delivered from wrath (1 Thess. 1:10; 5:9).	The unsaved will experience the wrath of God (Rev. 6:12–17).

Q 3. Will children be raptured with the Church?

A I have been asked this question many times in my meetings. One grandmother told me, "I have a two-year-old grandson, and although I am eager for the Rapture to take place, I would not like for him to go through the Tribulation." Many parents relate with that grandmother. I have preached for forty years that I believe children prior to the age of accountability are safe under the blood of the Lord Jesus Christ.

Dr. William L. Pettingill answered this question in these words: "I have no doubt that all who die in infancy, whether children of saved or of unsaved parents, are saved through the blood of Christ. . . . I am satisfied that all infants, since they are in a state of safety at the time of the Rapture, will be taken away with the Church.[5]

W. Myrddin Lewis wrote, "There can be no denying the grace and love of God in that moment, for when the trumpet will sound and the dead in Christ will arise, all the living believers, as well as all the world's little children, will be caught up together to meet the Lord in the air."[6]

In his book *Prophetic Questions Answered*, Keith L. Brooks wrote, "When our Lord comes, this world, ripened for judgment, will be deprived of the salt of the earth, the lights of the world and the innocent children. It will not be a question of little children being left behind, but of their parents, if they are not believers."[7]

Q 4. What will the people left after the Rapture think and do about those who have been raptured?

A Someone estimated that only 2 percent of the people living on earth at the time of the Rapture will be taken and that the other 98 percent will remain here. Of course, no one knows for sure. Just what those who are left will think and do we can only speculate.

I have a newspaper titled *The Last News*, which attempts to portray what newspapers might print immediately after the Rapture. Here are some of the possible headlines:

Christ Returns?
Millions Missing around the World
World Leaders Call for U. N. Emergency Session
Many Graves Found Open—Bodies Gone
Playful, Sensual World Shocked by Sudden Mass Kidnapping
Death Stalks the Highways
Throngs in the Nation Die of Heart Attacks
Weeping Mothers Cry, "Where is my baby?"
Stock Market Faces Crash
Thousands Attempt Suicide
Panic Stalks High School Corridors
Worldwide Business Paralyzed
Teenage Mobs Terrorize Cities[8]

These headlines can only speculate concerning what might happen after the Rapture. But one day—maybe today—Jesus will come for His elect. If you do not belong to Him, you will be left behind. You will have missed your opportunity (2 Thess. 2:10–12). Second Corinthians 6:2 states, "Now is the day of salvation." Acts 16:31 declares, "Believe on the Lord Jesus Christ, and thou shalt be saved."

Q 5. Will Christians who don't believe in the Rapture still be raptured?

A Some Christians do not know about the Rapture; others know about it but do not believe the Bible teaches it. When Christ comes, all Christians will be raptured: "We shall not all sleep, but we shall all be changed, in a moment, in the twinkling of an eye, at the last trump: for the trumpet shall sound, and the dead shall be raised incorruptible, and we shall be changed" (1 Cor. 15:51, 52). We are saved, not according to our views about the Rapture, but by grace through faith in the Lord Jesus Christ (Eph. 2:8, 9). If a person is truly saved, he will be raptured regardless of his belief concerning the Rapture. I would encourage anyone who says he doesn't believe in the Rapture to be like the Bereans who "searched the scriptures daily, whether those things were so" (Acts 17:11).

Q 6. Will our bodies disappear at the Rapture, or will they need burial plots?

A A Christian's body will disappear when the Rapture takes place. The Bible says, "We [Christians] shall not all sleep [die], but we shall all be changed, in a moment, in the twinkling of an eye, at the last trump: for the trumpet shall sound, and the dead shall be raised incorruptible, and we shall be changed" (1 Cor. 15:51, 52). Those of us believers living when Christ comes at the Rapture will not have to die. Our bodies will change in the twinkling of an eye (according to the General Electric Company, in 11/100 of a second), and we will get our glorified bodies. The Lord will "change our vile body, that it may be fashioned like unto his glorious body, according to the working whereby he is able even to subdue all things unto himself" (Phil. 3:21).

The Bible records that when God translated Enoch without seeing death, he "was not found" (Heb. 11:5). He disappeared and went to Heaven. When God translates the living Christians at the Rapture, we will not be found either. We will be with the Lord forever.

There will be no need for burial plots for our bodies. When salesmen have tried to sell me a burial plot, I have told them I do not expect to die. This statement arouses their curiosity, and they usually ask for an explanation. I tell them I expect Jesus Christ to come in my lifetime and that if He does, He will take me up to be with Him without dying. I am looking for the "Uppertaker," not the undertaker!

Q 7. What will happen to the animals left after the Rapture occurs?

A No animals will be raptured. Many pets will still have their owners, since in many cases families are composed of both believers and unbelievers. Those pets whose owners were raptured will probably find food for a while and will live off the food they can find. After a while many of them will starve to death because famine in the Tribulation will become extremely severe.

When the third seal is broken fairly early in the Tribulation, a measure of wheat will sell for a penny (Rev. 6:6). According to Thayer, a scholar of Greek, a measure is less than a quart. A measure of wheat would be one day's food and would satisfy a man with an average appetite. According to Matthew 20:2, a "penny" (denarius) is a day's wages. Dr. John Walvoord commented on these measurements: "To put it in ordinary language, the situation would be such that one would have to spend a day's wages for a loaf of bread with no money left to buy anything else."[9]

When the fourth seal is broken in the tribulation period, the fourth part of the earth will be killed with "sword, and with hunger, and with death, and with the beasts of the earth" (Rev. 6:8). The "sword" symbolizes war; "hunger" represents famine; "death" depicts pestilence; and "beasts of the earth" refers to animals that will kill people during the Tribulation. Perhaps the beasts of the earth (possibly wild animals) will kill people because of their hunger.

John Phillips has a different idea: "Another thought demands consideration. The beasts are closely linked with the pestilence, and this might be a clue. The most destructive creature on earth, so far as mankind is concerned, is not the lion or the bear, but the rat."[10]

Many animals will die after the Rapture when the twenty-one judgments come upon the earth, war and famine come (Rev. 6:4–6), the third part of trees and all green grass will burn (Rev. 8:7), the waters will turn to blood (Rev. 16:4), the sun will scorch with great heat (Rev. 16:8, 9), the great earthquake will shake the buildings to the ground all over the world (Rev. 16:18, 19) and hailstones weighing about 100 pounds will fall (Rev. 16:21).

A terrible time of tribulation is soon to come upon the world, upon both man and beast. The animals are unaware of what lies ahead, but you are aware. I pray that if you have not already done so, you will trust Jesus Christ as your personal Savior before He comes so that you will "escape all these things that shall come to pass, and to stand before the Son of man" (Luke 21:36).

Q 8. Which Scripture passages teach that people who heard the gospel before the Rapture cannot be saved after the Rapture?

A Paul wrote concerning both the coming of our Lord Jesus Christ and the revealing of Antichrist (2 Thess. 2:1, 8). He told about those who will perish because they did not receive the love of the truth so that they would be saved (v. 10). Then he stated, "And for this cause [not receiving the love of the truth] God shall send them strong delusion, that they should believe a lie [Greek, *the* lie; Antichrist is the lie]: that they all might be damned who believed not the truth, but had pleasure in unrighteousness" (vv. 11, 12).

Thomas L. Constable commented on this question: "The 'powerful delusion' (v. 11) that God will bring on these individuals in particular suggests that few if any then living on the earth will be saved after the Rapture. This seems to be a special judgment from God that will occur at this one time in history."[11]

Oliver B. Greene wrote the following statements concerning 2 Thessalonians 2:10–12: ". . . Let me emphasize the undeniable Bible fact that all who have heard the Gospel—all who have been exposed to the truth—*before the Rapture* will NOT be saved AFTER the Rapture. They will be sent strong delusion, they will believe The Lie, and *they ALL will be damned!*"[12]

I say to people in my meetings, "One second after the Rapture will be too late for anyone here to be saved if he has heard the gospel and rejected Jesus Christ." I repeat that statement now to you, the reader of this book. I would love to be able to say truthfully to you what Paul said to the Thessalonians: "But we are bound to give thanks alway to God for you, brethren beloved of the Lord, because God hath from the beginning chosen you to salvation through sanctification of the Spirit and belief of the truth: whereunto he called you by our gospel, to the obtaining of the glory of our Lord Jesus Christ" (2 Thess. 2:13, 14).

Q 9. Will the Antichrist be a Jew or a Gentile?

A Many people believe that the Antichrist will be a Jew. A number of prophetic scholars agree. Arthur W. Pink wrote, "The Antichrist will be a Jew."[13] Dr. Lehman Strauss, after quoting Daniel 11:37, concluded, "These words seem to indicate that the Antichrist will be an apostate Jew. It is not probable that one other than a Jew would present himself as being Israel's Messiah."[14] In his book *The End Times,* Herman A. Hoyt stated, "This raises the question concerning the racial origin of Antichrist. Though there is by no means any decisive answer, there are suggestions that he may be a Jew."[15]

Dr. Alva J. McClain wrote the following in his excellent book *Daniel's Prophecy of the Seventy Weeks:* "Some feel that the coming prince of Dan. 9:27 cannot also be the personal Antichrist, because the first is a Roman while the latter (they argue) must be a Jew. This, however, is no serious problem, for the same person could be a Roman *politically* and at the same time a Jew *racially."*[16]

Those who believe the Antichrist will be a Jew use Daniel 11:37 as proof: "Neither shall he regard the God of his fathers, nor the desire of women, nor regard any god: for he shall magnify himself above all." William W. Orr wrote in his book *A Simple Picture of the Future,* "Many believe he will be a Jew because of the scripture which says, 'he will not regard the God of his fathers.' "[17]

But Walter K. Price wrote, "This does not necessarily infer that the Antichrist is a Jew, for the word used here is Elohim—the general Semitic term for deity—and not Yahweh—the covenant God of Israel."[18]

In his booklet *Will the Antichrist Be a Jew?* Joseph Hoffman Cohn stated, "Will the Antichrist be a Jew? The immediate answer is that there is not a syllable in the Word of God that could justify such a speculation. . . ."[19] Then, after two pages of evidences, Hoffman wrote: "Thus is exploded the too-oft repeated error that Antichrist is to be a Jew. Quite on the contrary, this great monster that is to arise out of the sea will be a Gentile."[20]

A number of prophetic scholars concur that the Antichrist will be a Gentile:

J. Dwight Pentecost declared, "He is a Gentile. Since he arises from the sea (Rev. 13:1) and since the sea depicts the Gentile nations (Rev. 17:15), he must be of Gentile origin. He rises from the Roman empire, since he is a ruler of the people who destroyed Jerusalem" (Dan. 9:26).[21]

Richard W. DeHaan explained, "The Antichrist, then, will be the first beast of Revelation 13, a Gentile who comes forth from the nations and swiftly achieves world power."[22]

Dr. William Pettingill wrote, "The first of these characters is called, 'a beast out of the sea.' . . . Since, in Scripture imagery, the sea is a symbol of the Gentile nations, . . . it seems reasonable to conclude that the beast 'out of the sea' is a Gentile."[23]

S. Maxwell Coder came to the following conclusion:

Two statements in Revelation seem to make it evident that the beast is to be a Gentile. John wrote, "And I stood upon the sand of the sea, and saw a beast rise up out of the sea" (Rev. 13:1). This symbol of the sea may refer to the Gentile nations. . . . If the sea is indeed a symbol of the nations, . . . then the future world ruler will be a Gentile, not a Jew.[24]

God, through Daniel, revealed to us the nationality of the Antichrist: "The people of the prince that shall come shall destroy the city and the sanctuary" (Dan. 9:26). Daniel was predicting the destruction of Jerusalem and its temple by the soldiers of the Roman Empire, which took place in A.D. 70. Since the soldiers were "the people of the prince who shall come," the Antichrist will come from the area occupied by the Roman Empire.

Dr. David L. Cooper wrote:

What is meant by "the prince that shall come"? The only way to identify this one is to recognize the people who destroyed the city of Jerusalem in fulfillment of this prediction. All historians say that the Romans did it and that Titus was the general who finally destroyed the city. Since the Romans were the ones who captured Jerusalem, we may be certain that the prince to whom the reference is made is to be a Roman.[25]

It is obvious, then, that the Antichrist is of Roman origin. The proof of this argument could be stated as follows:

1. The "he" who makes a covenant and the "prince that shall come" are one and the same person.
2. They both have reference to the Antichrist.
3. The Antichrist is of the same nationality as the people who destroyed Jerusalem and the Temple.
4. The Romans destroyed Jerusalem and the Temple.
5. The Antichrist is of Roman origin.[26]

We conclude with J. Dwight Pentecost: "This destruction will be by the 'people of the *prince* that shall come.' The 'prince that shall come' is a Roman prince and the '*people* of the prince that shall come' would be the Romans."[27]

Q 10. Could the Antichrist possibly be Judas?

A Many have played the guessing game as to who will be the Antichrist. On the basis of a few verses in the New Testament, some people believe he will be Judas Iscariot. They use Luke 22:3 and John 13:27, which concern Satan's entering Judas. Then they use John 6:70 and 71, which call Judas a devil. John 17:12 calls him the "son of perdition," the name used in 2 Thessalonians 2:3 to refer to the Antichrist. We read that after Judas died, he went "to his own place" (Acts 1:25). Some believe this statement alludes to the bottomless pit where Judas has supposedly been for almost 2,000 years in preparation for his future role as the Antichrist. Dr. Kenneth S. Wuest, a scholar of Greek, wrote, "Judas will be the future Antichrist and is now in the Bottomless Pit."[28] Dr. M. R. DeHaan came to the same conclusion: "Judas, then, will be the Antichrist."[29] Dr. B. R. Lakin taught that the Antichrist will be Judas, and Dr. Oliver B. Greene held the same belief. Greene wrote in his book *Bible Prophecy*, "I believe that Judas Iscariot was the devil incarnate and that he will return to this earth as the Antichrist, the Man of Sin, 'son of perdition'!"[30] Nevertheless, I do not believe Judas will be the Antichrist, because Judas was a Jew and the Antichrist will be a Gentile.

Walter K. Price, in his book *The Coming Antichrist,* comes to a logical conclusion: "However, as interesting as this thesis is, it would mean that the Antichrist would be a Jew, and this is an improbable concession in the light of previous discussion. And since Judas certainly died (Acts 1:18), it would invest Satan with the power of resurrection, which is an impossible concession to make."[31]

In his book *Are These the Last Days?* Robert G. Gromacki explained why he does not believe Judas will be the Antichrist: "Since Judas was entered by Satan and was called by Jesus 'the son of perdition' (John 13:27; 17:12), they must be one and the same. However, there is no Scriptural basis for the teaching of human reincarnation. Judgment awaits man after death, not a second visit to the earth (Heb. 9:27)."[32]

Another prophetic scholar, W. Myrddin Lewis, agreed that Judas will not be the Antichrist: ". . . If the Antichrist is to be Judas, then we must accept the doctrine of reincarnation, as taught by some pagan religions, and also we must include in our own Christian doctrine a third resurrection. . . . To make Judas the Antichrist would be tantamount to teaching both these doctrines, and thus to be guilty of serious and grievous error. This we must reject as unscriptural."[33]

Q 11. Has the Antichrist already been born, and is he preparing to take his place in history?

A I believe the Antichrist might well be alive today. Since he will appear immediately after the Rapture as a full-grown man and since the Rapture itself is likely very near, he is probably living today.

Richard DeHaan agrees: "Is it possible that the future world dictator, the Antichrist, is now living somewhere upon this earth, unmindful of the role he will play on the world scene? . . . Some affirm that it is quite probable the future world dictator is now living."[34]

Thomas S. McCall and Zola Levitt wrote in their book *Satan in the Sanctuary,* "We might say that the Antichrist will have some Middle Eastern background and will rise in power on the European political scene. He might even be alive today."[35]

Dr. Bob Jones III concurs: "If the Rapture is upon us, the Antichrist is alive today. He is not yet revealed and will not be revealed until the Church is gone, but he would have to be a mature adult long before he appears as a world leader."[36]

Q 12. How will we know the Antichrist?

A The Antichrist will not be revealed until after the Rapture, so those of us believers living today will not know who he is. Paul wrote about the Antichrist (called in this passage "man of sin . . . son of perdition") in 2 Thessalonians 2:1–8. He explained that something is hindering the full outbreak of iniquity (v. 7). When that which is hindering is removed, "that Wicked [will] be revealed" (v. 8). The Holy Spirit in the Church is now holding back sin and lawlessness, but when He is "taken out of the way" (v. 7) at the Rapture of the Church, then the wicked one, the Antichrist, will be revealed to the world. Concerning this subject, Walter K. Price wrote, "Neither did the Lord intend the world to know who the Antichrist is until after the church is taken out at the rapture."[37]

Q 13. What country will the Antichrist come from?

A In the tribulation period ten kings will rule over the part of the world once occupied by the Roman Empire. A powerful ruler called the "little horn" (another name for the Antichrist) will arise among the ten kings and will subdue three of them (Dan. 7:7, 8, 24). Revelation 17:12 and 13 tell us that all ten kings will surrender to the Beast (Antichrist). Therefore, the Antichrist will come from one of the ten nations of Europe, and he will be their leader.

Q 14. Does the Antichrist know who he is?

A I do not believe the Antichrist will know the important part he will play. I again quote Richard DeHaan: "Is it possible that the future world dictator, the Antichrist, is now living somewhere upon this earth, *unmindful of the role he will play on the world scene* [emphasis mine]?"[38]

Dr. Louis Goldberg, in his book *Turbulence over the Middle East,* stated that the Antichrist will not know who he is: "No one will, at the point when the pact is made, be able to detect the ultimate design of power which this man will crave, and it is just possible that he himself will not realize the potential for evil of which he is capable."[39]

Q 15. What qualities will characterize the Antichrist, and what will eventually happen to him?

A The Bible has given the Antichrist many names that characterize him:

1. The little horn (Dan. 7:8)
2. The king of fierce countenance (Dan. 8:23)
3. The prince that shall come (Dan. 9:26)
4. The willful king (Dan. 11:36)
5. The man of sin (2 Thess. 2:3)
6. The son of perdition (2 Thess. 2:3)
7. That Wicked (or wicked) one (2 Thess. 2:8)
8. The Antichrist (1 John 2:18)
9. The Beast (Rev. 11:7—called the "beast" 36 times in Revelation)

The Bible also describes him:

1. He will be highly intelligent. He will have "eyes like the eyes of man" (Dan. 7:8), signifying intelligence; and he will understand "dark sentences" (Dan. 8:23), referring to his ability to interpret riddles.
2. He will be a great orator; he will have "a mouth speaking great things" (Dan. 7:8; Rev. 13:2, 5).
3. He will have a fierce appearance, for the Bible describes him as "a king of fierce countenance" (Dan. 8:23), which means he will have a strong and bold expression.
4. He will have mighty power. The Bible declares, "His power shall be mighty" (Dan. 8:24). According to Revelation 13:4, he will receive his power from the Devil, "the dragon [devil] which gave power unto the beast."
5. He will be destructive: "He shall destroy wonderfully . . . and shall destroy the mighty and the holy people" (Dan. 8:24).
6. He will be an extremely proud man: "He shall magnify himself" (Dan. 8:25); "he shall exalt himself, and magnify himself above every god" (Dan. 11:36).
7. He will be a clever politician: "And through his policy also he shall cause craft to prosper in his hand" (Dan. 8:25).
8. He will be a military genius: "And it was given unto him to make war with the saints, and to overcome them: and power

was given him over all kindreds, and tongues, and nations" (Rev. 13:7); "he went forth conquering, and to conquer" (Rev. 6:2).

9. He will be a materialistic pantheist: "But in his estate shall he honour the God of forces" (Dan. 11:38).

10. He will blaspheme: "And there was given unto him a mouth speaking great things and blasphemies. . . . And he opened his mouth in blasphemy against God, to blaspheme his name, and his tabernacle, and them that dwell in heaven" (Rev. 13:5, 6).

11. He will be lawless. The Bible refers to him as "that wicked" or lawless one (2 Thess. 2:8). It predicts, "The king shall do according to *his* [emphasis mine] will" (Dan. 11:36).

12. He will differ from all other men: "And they worshipped the beast, saying, Who is like unto the beast?" (Rev. 13:4).

13. He will be the wonder of the world. In *The End Times,* Hoyt wrote, "This man then will become the astonishment and wonder of the world. Differing from all others who have preceded him, possessing an amazing degree of high intelligence, demonstrating himself among men as no other demagogue before him."[40]

The Bible tells us what he will do:

1. He will be revealed after the Rapture (2 Thess. 2:7, 8).

2. He will subdue three kings (Dan. 7:8, 20, 24).

3. He'll control the Western bloc of ten countries (Rev. 17:12, 13).

4. He will confirm a covenant with the Jews for seven years (Dan. 9:27a).

5. He will break this covenant after three and one-half years (Dan. 9:27b).

6. He will have power over all the world for the last three and one-half years of the Tribulation (Rev. 13:5–7).

7. He will have an image of himself put into the temple at Jerusalem and will claim to be God (Rev. 13:14, 15; 2 Thess. 2:4).

8. He will persecute the Jews (Matt. 24:15–22; Rev. 13:4–7; Dan. 7:21, 25).

9. He will kill the two witnesses (Rev. 11:3–10).

10. He will blaspheme God (Rev. 13:5, 6).

11. He will change times and laws (Dan. 7:25).

12. He will demand universal worship (Rev. 13:12, 15).
13. He will have a deadly wound, but it will be healed (Rev. 13:3, 12).
14. He will cause everyone to receive a mark in his right hand or in his forehead, without which no one can buy or sell (Rev. 13:16, 17).
15. He will destroy the world church (Rev. 17:16, 17).

Finally, at the close of the tribulation period, he will come to his doom. Other wicked individuals have died horrible deaths by being drowned by water, burned by fire, eaten by dogs and worms, stricken with disease, hanged or swallowed alive by the earth, but the Antichrist will "come to his end," "broken without hand" by the Prince of Princes, the Lord Jesus Christ (Dan. 11:45; 8:25). Christ will consume him "with the spirit of his mouth" and destroy him "with the brightness of his coming" (2 Thess. 2:8).

At the Battle of Armageddon, which will be fought at the close of the Tribulation, the Antichrist and his armies will meet Jesus Christ and His armies from Heaven. The Beast (Antichrist) and false prophet will be cast alive into the Lake of Fire, which burns with brimstone (Rev. 19:20). The rest of his armies will be slain by the sword (God's Word), and the fowls will eat their flesh. Then at the close of the Millennium, the Devil will be cast into the Lake of Fire, where the Beast and false prophet are, and they "shall be tormented day and night for ever and ever" (Rev. 20:10). So "he shall come to his end, and none shall help him" (Dan. 11:45).

I close this section concerning the Antichrist with this warning given by Dr. Joseph M. Stowell in his booklet *Getting Ready for Antichrist:*

> *I must drop this word of warning to those of you who are unsaved. In 2 Thessalonians 2:8–12 we find these important warnings concerning Antichrist: "And then shall that Wicked be revealed, whom the Lord shall consume with the spirit of his mouth, and shall destroy with the brightness of his coming: Even him, whose coming is after the working of Satan with all power and signs and lying wonders, And with all deceivableness of unrighteousness in them that perish; because they received not the love of the truth, that they might be saved. And for this cause God shall send them strong delusion, that they should believe a lie: That they all might be damned who believed not the truth, but had pleasure in*

unrighteousness." You see, dear friend, if you have heard the gospel today, which you have, and refuse to accept Christ—if you should live until the Lord Jesus comes as the bright and morning Star to rapture away His Church in the air, you would not be caught away when Christ comes. You would be left upon the earth to go into the Great Tribulation.

You say, "Well, having seen such an event take place, I would certainly then believe on Christ." No, the Bible says you would not. You will be given over to believe the lie of Antichrist. He has turned the truth of God into a lie and the deceivableness of Satan, personified in Antichrist, will be of such a nature that you cannot help but believe it. It will be impossible for you to believe the gospel and be saved. Having heard the truth, if you go on in un-righteousness, you will not have another chance after Christ comes.

But you do have opportunity to be saved now. Why not turn to the Lord Jesus today? Today is the time—the accepted time. Tomorrow may be too late. Don't harden your heart any longer (Heb. 3:7 and 8). With all of your sins, fall at the Savior's feet and trust Him as your own. Remember, if you will open the door of your heart to Christ today, someday He will open the door of Heaven to you.[41]

Q 16. At the Judgment Seat of Christ, will Christ say, "Well done, thou good and faithful servant" to all Christians, even if they haven't been good and faithful?

A No, He will say, "Well done, thou good and faithful servant" only to Christians who have been good and faithful. Many of God's people are unfaithful, and their works are bad (2 Cor. 5:10). They will stand ashamed before Jesus Christ at the Judgment Seat of Christ (1 John 2:28). Their works will burn, and they will suffer loss (1 Cor. 3:15), a fact that means a great deal more than most people realize. The unfaithful Christian will lose the crowns offered to faithful Christians; he will lose the opportunity to rule in a place of authority during the Millennium; he will lose the commendation of the Savior. The unfaithful Christian ". . . shall re-ceive for the wrong which he hath done . . ." (Col. 3:25). Hebrews

13:17 states that he will feel great grief. Second John 8 tells us that believers can lose rewards, and Revelation 3:11 says we are to ". . . hold that fast which thou hast, that no man take thy crown."

Dr. Herbert Lockyer has challenged us with these words: "Faithfulness to the Lord and His Word is to form the basis of reward, as the Parable of the Talents makes clear. . . . If we want the Master's benediction and promotion to higher service, we must determine to be 'good and faithful' until the glorious Day breaks."[42]

Q 17. What happens to unfaithful Christians who have died? Are they rejoicing in Heaven now; will they later be ashamed at the Judgment Seat of Christ?

A I believe that many of God's children wonder about this question. Christians—unfaithful as well as faithful ones—go to Heaven when they die. Some people believe that in Heaven God will not bring up anything that we have done in this life. We sing the song "When We All Get to Heaven" by Eliza E. Hewitt: "When we all get to heaven, / What a day of rejoicing that will be! / When we all see Jesus, / We'll sing and shout the victory."

Dr. David Johnson, missionary statesman, said, "The older I get and the more I see Christians living like they are, the less I appreciate the song we sing about singing and shouting the victory. I am afraid there will be tears, remorse, and regret when we see Jesus."

I heard William McRae, a pastor from Canada and a former faculty member of Dallas Theological Seminary, answer a question similar to the one above. He answered with the following statements:

> I am personally of the opinion that a believer who dies during the time before the Rapture will stand before the Judgment Seat of Christ primarily so that what has been between him and God not confessed will be made straight. You see, it would be a tragic thing if something happened to someone in, say, the first century, who died as a believer out of fellowship with God with some sin that he refused to confess. . . . He has been now for 1,900 years in Heaven out of fellowship with the Lord. So it seems to me that what one would have to conclude then is that as he enters into Heaven he will go through the experience of the Judgment Seat of Christ so that his fellowship with the Lord will be what it ought to be.

In a doctoral dissertation at Bob Jones University titled *The Judgment Seat of Christ,* Thomas M. Meachum wrote:

> *The question of unconfessed sins, that is, those sins which the believer fails or refuses to confess even in the face of divine chastisement (Heb. 12:5–11), has been raised in regard to the Judgment Seat of Christ. To think a believer would be allowed into heaven at death and await his judgment with sins still on his account is certainly inconceivable and contrary to the glorified condition the New Testament presents of the believer who is "absent from the body" and "at home with the Lord" (2 Cor. 5:10). It must be concluded therefore that there must of necessity be a transformation that takes place in the believer's spiritual character at the moment he passes from the physical realm into the spiritual realm. Whether it be by confession or not (the Scriptures are silent on this point), a "making right" process must occur which restores complete fellowship between the believer and the Lord. . . . This does not mean that such a believer will not later be held accountable for his deeds at the Judgment Seat of Christ, but it does mean that the sin aspect has been removed.[43]*

May God help every believer to "abide in him; that, when he shall appear, we may have confidence, and not be ashamed before him at his coming" (1 John 2:28).

Q 18. How many Christians probably won't receive a crown?

A No one could accurately predict the percentage of Christians who will not receive a crown, but I believe we can estimate it better if we remember the reasons we will receive crowns.

Christians who run the Christian race well, who are temperate in all things, who bring their bodies into subjection will receive the *Incorruptible Crown* (1 Cor. 9:24–27). Many American Christians do not run the Christian race well. They are inordinately intemperate, and they let their bodily appetites rule them. I am afraid the percentage of those who will get this crown will be quite small.

Those who win others to Jesus Christ will receive the *Crown of Rejoicing* (1 Thess. 2:19, 20). I have read many times that at least 95 percent of Christians in America never win a soul to Jesus Christ, and most of them never try. So the percentage of those who receive this crown will be low.

Those who love the appearing of Jesus Christ will receive the *Crown of Righteousness* (2 Tim. 4:8). Some Christians pray the last prayer in the Bible: "Even so, come, Lord Jesus" (Rev. 22:20), but a higher percentage say, "My Lord delayeth his coming" (Luke 12:45) and consequently become careless in their living and do not look for His coming.

The *Crown of Life* will be given to those who endure temptations and trials and, in spite of them, still love the Lord (James 1:12). Too many Christians complain when trials and trouble come to them. They will not receive this crown.

Faithful pastors who feed the flock (not for money but of a ready mind), who do not lord it over God's heritage and who are good examples before their people will receive the *Crown of Glory* (1 Pet. 5:1–4). Thank God for faithful pastors, but many pastors are unfaithful!

Jeffrey K. Hadden reported the following facts concerning ministers in America.[44] From 67 percent to 95 percent of the ministers do not believe that the the Bible is the inspired, inerrant Word of God. From 51 percent to 97 percent of them do not believe that Adam and Eve were individual, real people. From 19 percent to 60 percent of them do not believe that Jesus was born of a virgin. These percentages show that many ministers—if we can rightly call them ministers—will receive no crowns.

John instructed belivers to "look to yourselves, that we lose not those things which we have wrought, but that we receive a full reward" (2 John 8). To receive a full reward, the crowns God has promised, we must run the Christian race well, win souls to Jesus Christ, love the appearing of Christ, love the Lord in spite of trials and temptations and be a faithful pastor. May God help each one of us to be that kind of person.

Q 19. What passage in the Bible indicates that the guillotine will be used during the Tribulation?

A We read of people in the coming tribulation period "... that were beheaded for the witness of Jesus, and for the word of God, and which had not worshipped the beast, neither his image, neither had received his mark upon their foreheads, or in their hands; and they lived and reigned with Christ a thousand years" (Rev. 20:4). These people will be saved in the tribulation period and will be beheaded because of their witness for Christ and the Word of God and their refusal to receive the mark of the Beast.

Revelation 6:9 mentions a similar group: "And when he had opened the fifth seal, I saw under the altar the souls of them that were slain for the word of God, and for the testimony which they held." Also, in Revelation 14:13 the apostle John wrote, "And I heard a voice from heaven saying unto me, Write, Blessed are the dead which die in the Lord from henceforth: Yea, saith the Spirit, that they may rest from their labours; and their works do follow them." According to a note at this verse in the Pilgrim Bible, "John is talking about those who die as martyrs during the *Great Tribulation*. Of course, it is true that all who die in the Lord are happy, yet these are to have special blessing because it will be harder during their lifetime to stand for the truth of God's Word than at any time in history."[45]

God has promised these martyrs that they shall live, which means that they will be resurrected at the close of the tribulation period and that they shall reign with Christ a thousand years (Rev. 20:4).

Q 20. Why do you think Petra will be the hiding place for Jews?

A Satan will persecute Israel during the last three and one-half years of the Tribulation. God has promised to protect Israel during that time and will prepare for her a place of safety. "And the woman [Israel] fled into the wilderness, where she hath a place prepared of God, that they should feed her there a thousand two hundred and threescore days" (Rev. 12:6; see also v. 14).

34

Many people believe God will use the ancient city of Petra to protect the Jews. Petra, the city of mystery, is located about fifty miles south of the Dead Sea in the land of Edom, now known as Jordan. It is approachable only through a narrow passage on the east, called the *Sik* (cleft), which is about a mile long. The rock of red sandstone towers to a height of 400 to 700 feet above the ground. In some places the way is so narrow that a person can almost touch the sides on either hand. A rivulet runs through its whole length. At the end of the *Sik* lies the Treasury of Pharaoh, a temple cut from the rock, with a remarkably preserved and beautifully sculptured 85-feet-tall facade. An amphitheater, formed entirely from the rock, is located two hundred yards farther along the valley. It is thirty-nine yards in diameter, with thirty-three tiers of seats accommodating from 3,000 to 4,000 spectators.

Petra at one time had 267,000 inhabitants and was a large market center. The Nabataeans occupied it from 100 B.C. until they were conquered by Rome about A.D. 106. It was a city of great riches and luxury. The armies of Mohammed swept down upon the city between A.D. 629 and 632. Soon afterward, its actual locality was completely lost. The explorer Burckhardt heard of it through an Arab and studied Arabic three years in order to go there disguised as a bedouin. He found Petra in 1812 and put it on the map again.

Daniel 11:41 tells us that Edom will escape from the Antichrist's hand when he goes south in his conquests. He will spare Edom, Moab and Ammon, and perhaps all the Transjordan territory will provide refuge for the persecuted Jews.

W. E. Blackstone, author of the popular book *Jesus Is Coming,* was so convinced that the Jews would flee to Petra that he arranged a caravan to take a large quantity of gospel literature to Petra and to store the material in caves and empty houses there. He sincerely believed that when the Jews go to Petra during the Tribulation, they will find those New Testaments and gospel tracts and through reading them will be saved by receiving Jesus Christ as their Messiah and Lord. May God grant it.

Q 21. Who will be the two witnesses referred to in Revelation 11?

A God never leaves Himself without a witness. In the tribulation period God will raise up two witnesses who will faithfully witness for Him. Based on the following reasons, most prophetic scholars agree that one of those witnesses will be Elijah: (1) he never died (2 Kings 2:9–11), and "it is appointed unto men once to die" (Heb. 9:27); (2) Malachi 4:5 and 6 predict that Elijah will appear on the earth to prepare the way for the coming of Christ to the earth; and (3) the Lord will give the witnesses power to perform the same miracle that Elijah performed in Old Testament days—withholding rain from the earth for three and one-half years (1 Kings 17:1; Luke 4:25; James 5:17, 18).

A number of commentators maintain that the second witness will be Moses. They base their belief on the facts that water will be turned into blood and plagues will be brought upon the earth, and Moses did both of those miracles in the Old Testament time.

However, I agree with Lehman Strauss, who wrote, "I am inclined to agree with those teachers who identify him [the second witness] as *Enoch*. . . . I believe that these two prophets, Enoch and Elijah, fit the case in Rev. 11 more accurately than any others."[46]

Q 22. Will anyone be saved during the tribulation period?

A This subject has confused some people. Some say that nobody will be saved after the Rapture. But the Bible makes it plain that a great multitude will be saved in the tribulation period. When the period begins, no Christians will be on the earth: they all will have been raptured. But God never leaves Himself without a witness. He will appoint two witnesses (Rev. 11:3) to preach God's Word to Jews and Gentiles. Then God will seal 144,000 Jews as His servants (Rev. 7:1–8), 12,000 from each of the twelve tribes of Israel.

After seeing this revelation, John saw "a great multitude, which no man could number, of all nations, and kindreds, and people, and tongues" (Rev. 7:9). Someone asked the question, "What are these which are arrayed in white robes?" The answer was given, "These are they which came out of great tribulation, and have washed their robes, and made them white in the blood of the Lamb" (Rev. 7:14).

Through the preaching of the two witnesses, the 144,000 Jews and the angel flying in the midst of Heaven (Rev. 14:6), a large number of Jews and Gentiles will be saved. J. Dwight Pentecost wrote concerning the basis of salvation in the Tribulation:

> *Salvation in the tribulation will certainly be on* the faith principle. . . .
>
> *The descriptions of the saved of the tribulation period make it perfectly plain that they were saved* by the blood *of the Lamb.* . . .
>
> *Salvation will be* by the work of the Holy Spirit. . . . [47]

Q 23. In the tribulation period, why won't everyone just take the mark of the Beast instead of being killed?

A If people in the Tribulation take the mark of the Beast, they will be lost forever. "And the third angel followed them, saying with a loud voice, If any man worship the beast and his image, and receive his mark in his forehead, or in his hand, the same shall drink of the wine of the wrath of God, which is poured out without mixture into the cup of his indignation; and he shall be tormented with fire and brimstone in the presence of the holy angels, and in the presence of the Lamb: And the smoke of their torment ascendeth up for ever and ever: and they have no rest day nor night, who worship the beast and his image, and whosoever receiveth the mark of his name" (Rev. 14:9–11).

If a person refuses the mark of the Beast, he will be subject to death. "And he [the false prophet] had power to give life unto the image of the beast, that the image of the beast should both speak, and cause that as many as would not worship the image of the beast should be killed" (Rev. 13:15).

If a person takes the mark, he is sure to be lost. But if he refuses the mark, he could possibly escape death, since some people will hide and will come to the end of the Tribulation unharmed. A number of people who are left at the Rapture will not have heard the gospel before Christ comes. They will hear it during the Tribulation and be saved. Some of them will be killed, but some will live and will be a part of the "sheep" to whom Christ will say, "Come, ye blessed of my Father, inherit the kingdom prepared for you from the foundation of the world" (Matt. 25:33, 34). They will rule and reign with Christ for a thousand years. If a person takes the mark, he will be in Hell forever and ever.

Q 24. When Jesus comes again, will He stand on the Mount of Olives, and will it split in two?

A Early in my Christian life, I heard a man tell a group of Christians, "You cannot find one verse in the Bible that says Christ will ever set His feet upon this earth again." Although I was a young Christian, I had already read this verse in the Bible: "And his feet shall stand in that day upon the mount of Olives, which is before Jerusalem on the east, and the mount of Olives shall cleave in the midst thereof toward the east and toward the west, and there shall be a very great valley; and half of the mountain shall remove toward the north, and half of it toward the south" (Zech. 14:4). Some time ago when I was preaching in a church in Ohio, a lady in the congregation arose from her seat, walked out into the aisle and said to me, "You won't find one verse in the whole Bible that says Christ will ever come back to this earth." I gave her the above verse as proof He shall indeed come again to this earth.

Just before Jesus Christ returned to Heaven after His resurrection, He stood on the Mount of Olives, less than a mile from Jerusalem. As He ascended, two men in white apparel said to His disciples, "Ye men of Galilee, why stand ye gazing up into heaven? This same Jesus, which is taken up from you into heaven, shall so come in like manner as ye have seen him go into heaven" (Acts 1:9–12). The Pilgrim Bible has a footnote at Acts 1:11: "This same Jesus shall come again in the same way that He went away. He went away in His glorified body. He will return in His glorified body. He went away as a Person. He will return as a Person. He was seen ascending. He will be seen descending. He was taken up in the clouds. He will return in the clouds."[48]

When Christ's feet touch the Mount of Olives, it will split in two, making a great valley, which the people of Israel will use as an avenue of escape to flee from Jerusalem.

Dr. J. Dwight Pentecost told an interesting story concerning his visit to the Mount of Olives. He said that a large hotel chain had commissioned research to be done concerning plans to build a hotel on the Mount of Olives. The researchers "reported that the site was a poor place to build because the Mount of Olives is the center of a geological fault and an earthquake in that area might divide the mount and a hotel would certainly be destroyed."[49]

Q 25. When will believers return to fight along with Jesus, and who will they fight against?

A Those of us who go up at the Rapture will immediately go to the Judgment Seat of Christ. At the close of the seven-year tribulation period, Christ will come from Heaven to earth at His revelation. The armies from Heaven—made up of the Church saints who have been raptured—and the angels of God will come with Him (see Matt. 25:31; 2 Thess. 1:7–10; Jude 14, 15; Rev. 19:14). When Christ comes to earth, He will judge those still living.

John recorded concerning this judgment: "And out of his mouth goeth a sharp sword [His Word], that with it he should smite the nations: and he shall rule them with a rod of iron: and he treadeth the winepress of the fierceness and wrath of Almighty God" (Rev. 19:15). We read further about the winepress in Revelation 14:20: "And the winepress was trodden without the city, and blood came out of the winepress, even unto the horse bridles, by the space of a thousand and six hundred furlongs" [200 miles]. Isaiah also spoke of the winepress: "I have trodden the winepress alone; and of the people there was none with me: for I will tread them in mine anger, and trample them in my fury; and their blood shall be sprinkled upon my garments, and I will stain all my raiment" (Isa. 63:3).

These verses refer to the Battle of Armageddon, which will be fought at the close of the Tribulation. The nations of the earth, from the north, south, east and west, will gather for this great battle. They will have been fighting among themselves, but when Christ comes from Heaven with His armies, they will band together to fight against Him. Revelation 19:19–21 describes this battle and its outcome: "And

39

I saw the beast, and the kings of the earth, and their armies, gathered together to make war against him that sat on the horse [Christ], and against his army [the saints of God]. And the beast was taken, and with him the false prophet. . . . These both were cast alive into a lake of fire burning with brimstone. And the remnant [the rest of them] were slain with the sword [Word] of him that sat upon the horse, which sword proceeded out of his mouth: and all the fowls were filled with their flesh."

We believers will return to earth with Christ at the close of the Tribulation as part of His army, but He will do all the fighting. Isaiah 63:3 records what He will say: "I have trodden the winepress alone; and of the people there was none with me." His statement, "There was none with me," means that no one will help Him execute the judgment; He will act alone. Of course, many people will be with Him as spectators. He will fight "the beast, and the kings of the earth, and their armies" (Rev. 19:19), His enemies from all over the world.

The psalmist wrote, "By the word of the LORD were the heavens made; and all the host of them by the breath of his mouth" (Ps. 33:6). John recorded, "And out of his mouth goeth a sharp sword, that with it he should smite the nations" (Rev. 19:15). Therefore, the Lord Jesus gives life through His words and also brings death through His words.

The answer to the question asked in Revelation 13:4, "Who is like unto the beast? who is able to make war with him?" will be answered: The Lord Jesus Christ, King of Kings and Lord of Lords.

God invites the people of this earth to "be wise now therefore, O ye kings: be instructed, ye judges of the earth. Serve the Lord with fear, and rejoice with trembling. Kiss the Son, lest he be angry, and ye perish from the way, when his wrath is kindled but a little. Blessed are all they that put their trust in him" (Ps. 2:10–12).

If you haven't already done it, "kiss the Son" (which means receive Him as Savior, worship Him, honor Him, love Him and obey Him).

Q 26. Since most Jews don't believe in Christ, when the tribulation period ends, will they or can they be saved?

A Most of the Jews living today do not believe on the Lord Jesus Christ and are unsaved. Thank God for those Jews who have received the Lord Jesus Christ as their personal Savior. Quite a number of Jews will be saved in the tribulation period following the Rapture. About 144,000 will be saved and sealed as the servants of God (Rev. 7:1–8). God will use them as His witnesses to reach others for Christ. He will save two witnesses to prophesy for 1,260 days in the Tribulation (Rev. 11:3). Some Jews will accept Christ as their Savior as a result of the witness of the 144,000 (Rev. 7:9–14).

When Jesus Christ judges the Jews when He gathers them at the Second Advent, He will purge out the rebels (Ezek. 20:33–38). One-third of them will come through the testing and will call on the name of the Lord. In Zechariah 13:9, God declares, "I will hear them: I will say, It is my people: and they shall say, The LORD is my God." Zechariah wrote concerning the repentance of the Jews when they see Christ: "And I will pour upon the house of David, and upon the inhabitants of Jerusalem, the spirit of grace and of supplications: and they shall look upon me whom they have pierced, and they shall mourn for him, as one mourneth for his only son, and shall be in bitterness for him, as one that is in bitterness for his firstborn" (Zech. 12:10). They will mourn because of what they did to Christ at His first coming.

God also promises that when He gathers them out of all countries and takes them to their own land, "Then will I sprinkle clean water upon you, and ye shall be clean: from all your filthiness, and from all your idols, will I cleanse you. A new heart also will I give you, and a new spirit will I put within you: and I will take away the stony heart out of your flesh, and I will give you an heart of flesh" (Ezek. 36:25, 26).

Isaiah told us what the Jews will say when they meet Christ: "And it shall be said in that day, Lo, this is our God; we have waited for him, and he will save us: this is the LORD; we have waited for him, we will be glad and rejoice in his salvation" (Isa. 25:9).

Paul wrote in Romans 11:26: "And so all Israel shall be saved: as it is written, There shall come out of Sion the Deliverer, and shall turn away ungodliness from Jacob."

Lewis Sperry Chafer commented on the phrase "all Israel": " 'All

Israel' of Romans 11:26 is evidently that separated and accepted Israel that will have stood the divine judgments which are yet to fall upon that nation (cf. Matt. 24:37—25:13). The Apostle distinguishes clearly between Israel the nation and a spiritual Israel (cf. Rom. 9:6; 11:1–36)."[50]

Therefore, the answer to the question, Will they or can they be saved? is *Yes.* Many Jews who had not heard the gospel before the Rapture will be saved in the tribulation period.

Q 27. In Matthew 24:31, who are the elect that the angels will gather together?

A Matthew 24:31 states: "And he shall send his angels with a great sound of a trumpet, and they shall gather together his elect from the four winds, from one end of heaven to the other." This verse refers to the gathering of the people of Israel from the four corners of the earth back to their own land at the close of the tribulation period when Christ comes to reign on the earth.

God has made many promises to gather them and take them back to their land:

> *And it shall come to pass, when all these things are come upon thee, the blessing and the curse, which I have set before thee, and thou shalt call them to mind among all the nations, whither the* Lord *thy God hath driven thee, And shalt return unto the* Lord *thy God, and shalt obey his voice according to all that I command thee this day, thou and thy children, with all thine heart, and with all thy soul; that then the* Lord *thy God will turn thy captivity, and have compassion upon thee, and will return and gather thee from all the nations, whither the* Lord *thy God hath scattered thee. If any of thine be driven out unto the outmost parts of heaven, from thence will the* Lord *thy God gather thee, and from thence will he fetch thee: And the* Lord *thy God will bring thee into the land which thy fathers possessed, and thou shalt possess it; and he will do thee good, and multiply thee above thy fathers. And the* Lord *thy God will circumcise thine heart, and the heart of thy seed, to love the* Lord *thy God with all thy soul, that thou mayest live (Deut. 30:1–6).*

Therefore, behold, the days come, saith the Lord, that they shall no more say, The Lord liveth, which brought up the children of Israel out of the land of Egypt; But, The Lord liveth, which brought up and which led the seed of the house of Israel out of the north country, and from all countries whither I had driven them; and they shall dwell in their own land (Jer. 23:7, 8).

When I have brought them again from the people, and gathered them out of their enemies' lands, and am sanctified in them in the sight of many nations; then shall they know that I am the Lord their God, which caused them to be led into captivity among the heathen: but I have gathered them unto their own land, and have left none of them any more there (Ezek. 39:27, 28).

Q 28. When Christ returns and sets up His thousand-year reign, what will happen to those who have survived the Tribulation?

A When Christ comes to earth at the close of the tribulation period, He will gather those who are still living to judge them. He will gather the Jews in the wilderness to determine who among them may enter the Millennium. He will purge out the rebels and will not allow them to enter the millennial reign (Ezek. 20:33–38). He will, however, allow one-third of the Jews to go into the Millennium (Zech. 13:8, 9).

The Gentiles will also be gathered for judgment, to see who will enter the Millennium. Christ will come to earth in His glory and will sit on His throne (Matt. 25:31), judging all nations and separating the "sheep" from the "goats" (Matt. 25:32). The word for "nations," *ethnos,* can be translated "Gentiles." Christ will judge on an individual basis, not national. He will put the sheep, the saved ones, on His right hand and the goats, the lost ones, on His left hand (Matt. 25:33). He will say to the sheep, "Come, ye blessed of my Father, inherit the kingdom prepared for you from the foundation of the world" (Matt. 25:34).

He will say further, "For I was an hungred, and ye gave me meat: I was thirsty, and ye gave me drink: I was a stranger, and ye took me in: Naked, and ye clothed me: I was sick, and ye visited me: I was in prison, and ye came unto me" (Matt. 25:35, 36). The righteous will ask how they ministered to Him (Matt. 25:37–39). He will answer, "Inasmuch as ye have done it unto one of the least of these my brethren, ye have done it unto me" (Matt. 25:40). In order to understand what Christ taught in these verses, we need to know that "brethren" here refers to Jews; in other words, to the 144,000 witnesses who will take the gospel to the people of the earth during the Tribulation (Rev. 7:1–17). These witnesses will refuse the mark of the Beast and therefore will be unable to buy or sell (Rev. 13:17). As a result, they will be hungry, pursued by the authorities and cast unto prison. Only people who have believed their message and have been saved by the Lord Jesus Christ will help them. These saved people will demonstrate their faith by providing for the physical and material needs of the witnesses. They will not be saved because they feed, clothe, house and visit the servants of God, but they will do these acts because they have been saved. They will show their faith by their works.

Then Christ will say to those on the left, "Depart from me, ye cursed, into everlasting fire, prepared for the devil and his angels" (Matt. 25:41). They demonstrated their rejection of the message of salvation by their lack of works, and they "shall go away into everlasting punishment" (Matt. 25:42, 43, 46). But the righteous—those who have believed the message and received the Savior—will go into life eternal (Matt. 25:46b).

Concerning the coming judgment of the sheep and the goats, J. Dwight Pentecost came to the following conclusion: When Jesus comes, He will come as the Judge. He will ask one question: What did you do with the salvation I offered you? Pentecost continued, "He will test all men's response to this offer of salvation. Those who have received it will be received into His kingdom. Those who have rejected it will be excluded from His kingdom. The issue is very clear; there is no middle ground."[51]

Q 29. Do you agree that men must rebuild a physical temple where the Dome of the Rock now stands?

A According to the Word of God, a temple will be rebuilt in Jerusalem. It will be rebuilt on Mount Moriah, where Abraham offered Isaac to the Lord (Gen. 22:1, 2), which David purchased and on which he built an altar to the Lord (2 Sam.

24:18–25; 1 Chron. 21:18–30), where Solomon built the first temple (2 Chron. 3:1, 2) and where Zerubbabel built the second temple (Ezra 1; 4:3; 5:15; 6:3), which Herod later remodeled. The temple could not be rebuilt somewhere else in Jerusalem because according to the law of Moses, only the ancient site is permissible for the temple (Deut. 12:10–14).

A Moslem shrine, the Dome of the Rock, now occupies the area where the temple is to be rebuilt. During the Six-day War in 1967, Israel took from Jordan the city of Old Jerusalem, where the temple mount is located. People have speculated as to how the Dome of the Rock will be removed in order for the Tribulation temple to be built there. Suggestions include the following: an earthquake, a fire or sabotage could destroy it; it could be destroyed in a war; or it could be relocated. But another possibility exists, as a visitor to Israel discovered during a discussion with his Jewish guide:

> I pointed out how impossible it would be to remove the Dome of the Rock and replace it with a structure built by the Jews.
>
> "But there is no need to replace the Dome of the Rock," he told me. "The ancient temple of Solomon did not sit on the spot where the Moslem mosque is now located. It was to the west."
>
> He pointed to a vast area directly west of the Dome of the Rock. It is perfectly flat, paved with huge stones, and there would be room enough here for several large buildings.
>
> Then the guide explained, "The temple of Solomon was not built over the rock on which Abraham sacrificed Isaac. It was to the west of this rock. The rock itself was in the court of the temple and was the place where the altar of incense was placed. This altar, often called 'the great altar,' was erected on top of the stone, and we can still see today the channels cut into the stone and the place below where the blood of the sacrifices was drained off and flowed down to the Kidron Brook in the valley below. So, if a new temple is built by the Jews on the exact site of the temple of Solomon, it will be to the west of the Dome of the Rock, and there is no need to tear down the Dome of the Rock. The two buildings can stand side by side on Mount Moriah.

*With numbers of Jewish people everywhere in the world devoutly
hoping and praying for the rebuilding of their sacred temple, and
with the great area west of the Dome of the Rock available for such
a building, it does not seem impossible that the Jews and Arabs
could make an agreement whereby both could have their sacred
buildings, and could share this historic mountain top in Jerusalem.*[52]

We read in Revelation 11:1: "And there was given me a reed like
unto a rod: and the angel stood, saying, Rise, and measure the temple
of God, and the altar, and them that worship therein." This verse
definitely states that there will be a temple in the coming tribulation
period. God also tells us, "Who opposeth and exalteth himself above all
that is called God, or that is worshipped; so that he as God sitteth in
the temple of God, shewing himself that he is God" (2 Thess. 2:4). This
description refers to the Antichrist (or "man of sin" or "son of perdition," v. 3), who in the middle of the coming tribulation period will
demand the worship that belongs to God.

The Jews recite the following prayer three times a day: "May it be
Thy will that the Temple be speedily rebuilt in our days."

Dr. Gerald Stover wrote concerning the temple: "*Time* magazine
raised the question: 'Should the Temple be rebuilt?' Various religious
and political reasons are given as obstacles in the way of rebuilding the
temple, and while these are interesting they have nothing to do with
the fulfillment of Scripture. God says it will be rebuilt."[53]

Q 30. If someone hears the gospel and does not accept
Christ as his Savior, enters the tribulation period and
refuses the mark of the beast, will his refusal save him?

A If a person hears the gospel and rejects Christ before the
Rapture, his destination will be settled: he will be lost
forever, even if he refuses to take the mark of the Beast.
According to 2 Thessalonians 2:10–12, those who hear the truth but
do not receive the love of the truth will perish; God will send them
strong delusion; they will believe the Devil's lie; and they will all be
damned or condemned.

Let me plead with you right now to trust the Lord Jesus Christ
as your personal Savior before He comes. "Behold, now is the accepted
time; behold, now is the day of salvation" (2 Cor. 6:2). One second after

He comes will be too late for those who have heard the truth and rejected it.

Q 31. Who is the woman in Revelation 12:1?

A Revelation 12:1 says, "And then appeared a great wonder in heaven; a woman clothed with the sun, and the moon under her feet, and upon her head a crown of twelve stars." The word "wonder" in this verse can be translated "sign," so we know that this great sign represents something else.

Genesis 37:9–11 relates a similar use of symbols. In the Genesis passage, the sun and the moon represent Jacob and Rachel, and the eleven stars represent the sons of Jacob. Jacob realized these symbols represented his entire family, Israel, "of whom as concerning the flesh Christ came" (Rom. 9:5). The woman in Revelation 12:1 represents the nation of Israel.

Revelation 12:2 pictures the woman laboring in birth and awaiting the delivery of her child, who symbolizes Christ, while the dragon, the Devil, stands ready to devour Him as soon as he is born (v. 4). This reference alludes to Herod's attempt to destroy the baby Jesus (Matt. 2:16). The woman identified as Israel will bring forth a man child, who will "rule all nations with a rod of iron" (Rev. 12:5). The man child is the Lord Jesus Christ. Psalm 2:9 predicts, "Thou [Christ] shalt break them with a rod of iron," and in Revelation 19:15 God declares, ". . . He [Christ] shall rule them with a rod of iron."

Revelation 12:5 says, ". . . Her child was caught up unto God, and to his throne," which represents Christ's ascension to Heaven following His life on earth. Between verses 5 and 6, the Church period occurs. Verse 6 describes the woman's (Israel's) flight into the wilderness for 1,260 days (the last half of the Tribulation) to a place prepared by God in order to protect her. Verses 7 through 17 tell about a war in Heaven, the casting from Heaven of Satan and his angels, and the persecution of Israel. God will be with Israel during this time. Notice what He will do:

• He will prepare a place in the wilderness for her (Rev. 12:6).
• He will feed her (Rev. 12:6).

- He will give her two wings of a great eagle (Rev. 12:14; cf. Exod. 19:4; Deut. 32:11, 12).
- He will nourish her (Rev. 12:14).
- He will help her (Rev. 12:16).
- He will cause the flood (symbolically "representing whatever means of destruction Satan, working through the Antichrist, will bring against Israel during the last half of the tribulation"[54]) to be swallowed up (Rev. 12:16).

Dr. Henry Morris wrote concerning this flood: "The overflowing horde of men and weapons sent after the Jews in the wilderness by the beast . . . though infinitely superior to the unarmed refugees in might, is utterly unable to conquer them or even to reach them."[55]

Q 32. Will children be born during the Millennium?

A Yes. The Bible informs us that during the Millennium children will be born. Referring to millennial glory, God's Word says, "There shall yet old men and old women dwell in the streets of Jerusalem, and every man with his staff in his hand for very age. And the streets of the city shall be full of boys and girls playing in the streets thereof" (Zech. 8:4, 5). Again, God informs us concerning how the land will be divided among the Jews in the coming Millennium; then He instructs Israel: "And it shall come to pass, that ye shall divide it by lot for an inheritance unto you, and to the strangers that sojourn among you, which *shall beget children* among you: and they shall be unto you as born in the country among the children of Israel; they shall have inheritance with you among the tribes of Israel" (Ezek. 47:22; italics added).

William W. Orr wrote concerning life in the Millennium: "Romance will take up again, families will be formed. Children will be born. . . . Babies will grow up. Children will be strong. Young people will marry with joy. The population will swell mightily. . . . The earth will ring with the laughter of children."[56]

Q
33. Will the Church dwell on earth during the Millennium or in a city above the earth?

A
At least three theories exist concerning where the Church will dwell during the Millennium. Some say the Church-age saints will live *on earth* in their glorified bodies. Some have criticized this view. G. L. Murray, in his book *Millennial Studies,* wrote, "Premillennialism makes no provision for the reconciliation of such irreconcilables as resurrected saints and mortal sinners in the same society."[57] But these aspects are not irreconcilable. Christ lived on earth in His glorified body during the forty days between His resurrection and ascension. He ate with His disciples and talked many times with people. Also, the Old Testament saints who rose from the dead shortly after His resurrection lived here on earth for a short time.

Some Bible scholars believe the resurrected saints will live *in the New Jerusalem* during the Millennium. J. Dwight Pentecost taught this point of view and wrote, "If such an interpretation be correct, there would be a solution to the perplexing problem that arises from placing resurrected saints on the earth to mingle freely with the unresurrected during the millennium."[58]

Still others take the view that *Heaven* will be the abode of glorified saints during the Millennium. Alva J. McClain believed this view and considered the great distance between Heaven and earth no problem, since the glorified saints will have the power to go from earth to Heaven or from Heaven to earth instantly. He believed that saints could live in Heaven and still have access to the earth to serve the Lord Jesus Christ in whatever capacities He assigned them.[59]

Leon J. Wood summarized the issue in this way: "A final, certain answer is not forthcoming. The Scriptures simply do not say where glorified saints will live. Any of the three suggestions made, however, qualify as possibilities."[60]

Q 34. What type of worship, lifestyles and activities will occur during the Millennium?

A During the Millennium, the whole world will unite to worship God and His Son, the Lord Jesus Christ, as we learn from three Old Testament references: "And it shall come to pass, that from one new moon to another, and from one sabbath to another, shall all flesh come to worship before me, saith the LORD" (Isa. 66:23). "For then will I turn to the people a pure language, that they may all call upon the name of the Lord, to serve him with one consent" (Zeph. 3:9). "And it shall come to pass, that every one that is left of all the nations which come against Jerusalem shall even go up from year to year to worship the King, the LORD of hosts, and to keep the feast of tabernacles" (Zech. 14:16).

As for the lifestyles and activities during the Millennium, S. Maxwell Coder wrote,

A study of all that is revealed about life in the golden age shows people will marry, have children, and get old. They will work, sing, play, worship, and fall into sin. Some will rebel against the Lord. Men will operate farms, keep sheep, go fishing, build and repair homes, and engage in manufacturing. They will travel by highway and by ship. They will serve God, bear witness for him, and offer sacrifices in the temple at Jerusalem. They will eat, drink, sleep, and live in houses. There will be cities and nations.[61]

Q 35. How long will Christ reign?

A Revelation 20:6 says that those who will take part in the first resurrection ". . . shall reign with him a thousand years." Luke 1:33 declares, "And he shall reign over the house of Jacob for ever; and of his kingdom there shall be no end." I answered this question in an earlier book.

The Bible teaches that Christ will reign on this earth for one thousand years. This is known as the millennium. Many times the

Scriptures say that Christ will reign forever (Isa. 9:6, 7; Dan. 7:13, 14; Luke 1:30–33; Rev. 11:15). Some see a problem here. John Calvin said the thousand-year reign of Christ nullified the eternal reign of Christ. He said of those who limit the reign of Christ to one thousand years: *"their fiction is too puerile to require or deserve refutation"* (Institutes of the Christian Religion, II, pp. 250, 251). *Christ will sit on "the throne of his father David" (Luke 1:32) for one thousand years when the "kingdoms of this world are become the kingdoms of our Lord, and of his Christ" (Rev. 11:15). When the one thousand years are completed, Christ will deliver up "the kingdom to God, even the Father; when he shall have put down all rule and all authority and power. For he must reign, till he hath put all enemies under his feet. The last enemy that shall be destroyed is death. . . . And when all things shall be subdued unto him, then shall the Son also himself be subject unto him that put all things under him, that God may be all in all" (1 Cor. 15:24–28).*[62]

Dr. Alvin J. McClain, in *The Greatness of the Kingdom*, made the following statements:

When the last enemy of God has been put down by our Lord acting as Mediatorial King, the purpose of His Mediatorial Kingdom will have been fulfilled [I Cor. 15:25, 26]. . . .

. . . The Mediatorial Kingdom of our Lord ends, not by abolition, but by its mergence into the Universal Kingdom of God. Thus it is perpetuated forever, no longer as a separate entity, but in indisoluble union with the original Kingdom of God from which it sprang [I Cor. 15:24, 28]. . . . This does not mean the end of our Lord's regal activity, but rather that from here onward in the unity of the Godhead He reigns with the Father as the eternal Son. There is no longer two thrones: one His Messianic throne and the other the Father's throne [Rev. 22:3–5; cf. 3:21]. . . .[63]

Q 36. At the end of the thousand years, will the bodies of the remaining people be changed into glorified bodies?

A I have often thought about this question, but I have never found any clear Scripture to answer it. The children born in the Millennium who come to the end of that period and do not rebel against Christ will probably be changed in the same way as we Christians will be at the Rapture. Dr. John F. Walvoord wrote, "It is assumed, though the Scriptures do not state it, that the millennial saints at the end of the millennium will be translated prior to their entrance into the eternal state and thus will qualify for entrance into the heavenly Jerusalem."[64]

Dr. Herman A. Hoyt presented a quite different thought:

From the reading of the text, it appears they have access to the New Jerusalem but will live in the broad expanse of the restored earth. It would also seem that they live in natural bodies in which there is no longer any sin nature, as Adam once was before the fall, and as Christ lived during the days of His flesh (Heb. 4:15; 2 Cor. 5:21). . . .[65]

Q 37. What is the difference between Hell and the Lake of Fire?

A Some people are confused concerning Hell, so I think it would help to explain what the Bible teaches on the subject.

The New Testament uses three Greek words that are translated into English by the one word "hell": *tartarus, hades* and *gehenna.*

The word *tartarus* occurs only once in the New Testament: "For if God spared not the angels that sinned, but cast them down to *hell,* and delivered them into chains of darkness, to be reserved unto judgment" (2 Pet. 2:4). The word "hell" here is a translation of the verb form *tartarus,* and it refers to a pit of darkness that serves as a prison house for certain angels who rebelled against God. Jude 6 also describes them: "And the angels which kept not their first estate, but left their own habitation, he hath reserved in everlasting chains under darkness unto the judgment of the great day." These fallen angels are reserved under darkness awaiting their judgment, which will take place when God judges their leader, the Devil (Rev. 20:10), and He will cast the Devil and them "into everlasting fire, prepared for the devil and his angels" (Matt. 25:41).

In Luke 16:19–31 we find Jesus telling the story of two men who died—the rich man and Lazarus. Both of them went to *hades,* which at that time was divided into two compartments, one a place of torment (vv. 23, 24, 28) and the other a place of comfort (v. 25). A "great gulf [was] fixed" between the two compartments (v. 26), and although they could see each other, the people in each section could not pass from one section to the other.

The section of *hades* that the righteous dead went into was called "Abraham's bosom" (Luke 16:22) and "paradise." Jesus told the repentant dying thief, "To day shalt thou be with me in paradise" (Luke 23:43), indicating that at death He went to Paradise, and so did the thief who was saved. At that time Paradise was in the heart of the earth (Matt. 12:40), but when Jesus Christ rose from the dead, He opened the Paradise section of *hades* and took the Old Testament saints into Heaven. We read about this event in Ephesians 4:8–10: "Wherefore he saith, When he ascended up on high, he led captivity captive, and gave gifts unto men. (Now that he ascended, what is it but that he also descended first into the lower parts of the earth? He that descended is the same also that ascended up far above all heavens, that he might fill all things.)" Notice that "he descended first into the lower parts of the earth" (*hades* or *sheol*) (v. 9), and then He "ascended up on high" and "led captivity captive" (v. 8). One translation reads, "He led a multitude of captives," and it refers to the fact that at His ascension into Heaven, Jesus Christ led out the multitude of Old Testament saints who had been in the part of *hades* called Abraham's bosom or Paradise.

The last of the three words translated by the English word "hell" is *gehenna.* This word refers to the final Hell to which every lost soul will be consigned for all eternity. It is found twelve times in the New Testament (Matt. 5:22, 29, 30; 10:28; 18:9; 23:15, 33; Mark 9:43, 45, 47; Luke 12:5; James 3:6). Note that out of the twelve occurrences of this word in the New Testament, Jesus used it eleven times.

The following chart shows every New Testament occurrence of the word "hell."

HADES (ten times)	TARTARUS (one time)	GEHENNA (twelve times)
Matthew 11:23	2 Peter 2:4	Matthew 5:22
Matthew 16:8		Matthew 5:29, 30
Luke 10:15		Matthew 10:28
Luke 16:23		Matthew 18:9
Acts 2:27, 31		Matthew 23:15, 33
Revelation 1:18		Mark 9:43
Revelation 6:8		Mark 9:45
Revelation 20:13, 14		Mark 9:47
		Luke 12:5
		James 3:6

Gehenna, the Lake of Fire and the second death are synonymous. Five times in the New Testament we read of the Lake of Fire (Rev. 19:20; 20:10; 20:14; 20:15; 21:8).

Right now no one is in this final place of punishment. The first occupants of this awful place will be the Beast and the false prophet as described in Revelation 19:20: "And the beast was taken, and with him the false prophet that wrought miracles before him, with which he deceived them that had received the mark of the beast, and them that worshipped his image. These both were cast alive into a lake of fire burning with brimstone."

The Devil and his angels will be cast into the final Hell next. After that event, the Great White Throne Judgment, described in Revelation 20:11–15, will take place. Then all the wicked dead who have been resurrected and judged will be "cast into the lake of fire." Notice that death and hell *(hades)* will be cast into the Lake of Fire (Rev. 20:14). "Death" here refers to the grave, which had received the body, and "hell" refers to *hades,* which had received the soul. Both body and soul will be cast into the Lake of Fire.

Jesus Christ said that the everlasting fire was "prepared for the devil and his angels" (Matt. 25:41). This everlasting fire was not intended for mankind. If a person goes there, it will be because he chose to do so by refusing God's gracious offer of eternal life. Jesus made this fact plain: "And ye will not come to me, that ye might have life" (John 5:40). He promised, "All that the Father giveth me shall come to me; and him that cometh to me I will in no wise cast out" (John 6:37). Nobody can ever blame God for sending him to Hell. He is "not willing that any should perish, but that all should come to repentance" (2 Pet. 3:9).

I once read a story about an old saloon called the Gates of Hell, which was located near Calvary Church in Chicago. Someone asked a young man for directions to the saloon. "Just go right by Calvary, and you will come to the Gates of Hell," the young man explained. Likewise, if you go by Calvary, where Jesus died, and do not trust Him as your personal Savior, you too will come to the Gates of Hell. They will close on you, and forever you will be separated from God. As Danté wrote, you must "abandon all hope, ye who enter here."

Q 38. If there is fire in Hell, how could Hell be dark?

A There definitely is fire in Hell.
  • Eternal fire (Jude 7)
  • Everlasting fire (Matt. 18:8; 25:41)
• Furnace of fire (Matt. 13:42, 50)
• Hellfire (Matt. 5:22; 18:9; Mark 9:47; James 3:6)
• Fire and brimstone (Luke 17:29; Rev. 14:10; 20:10; 21:8)
• Lake of Fire (Rev. 19:20; 20:10, 14, 15; 21:8)
• Unquenchable fire (Matt. 3:12; Mark 9:43–46, 48; Luke 3:17)
  Hell is definitely dark:
• Cast into outer darkness (Matt. 8:12; 22:13)
• Mist of darkness reserved forever (2 Pet. 2:17)
• Blackness of darkness reserved forever (Jude 13)

According to *Vine's Expository Dictionary of New Testament Words,* the Greek word Peter and Jude used for darkness is *zophos,* which "denotes the gloom of the nether world; hence, thick darkness, darkness that may be felt."[66]

The ninth plague God sent upon the Egyptians was a thick darkness. "And the LORD said unto Moses, Stretch out thine hand toward heaven, that there may be darkness over the land of Egypt, even darkness which may be felt. And Moses stretched forth his hand toward heaven; and there was a thick darkness in all the land of Egypt three days: They saw not one another, neither rose any from his place for three days: but all the children of Israel had light in their dwellings" (Exod. 10:21–23). This darkness was similar to the darkness of Hell— a darkness that they could feel, a darkness that kept them from seeing each other or even rising from their places. It lasted only three days, but the darkness in Hell will last forever. Think of a place without the sun, the moon or stars and without an electric light, a lamp light, candlelight or even a lightning bug—only forever darkness. This horrible darkness is the reservation for the wicked. Seeing people in this life drifting with no purpose is difficult, but knowing that this aimlessness and darkness will extend throughout all eternity is so awful that the mind cannot dwell upon it very long.

Jesus spoke of those who "loved darkness rather than light, because their deeds were evil" (John 3:19), and since they hate the light (John 3:20), they will get darkness forever.

Robert L. Sumner reported the following account:

I remember hearing the noted evangelist and university founder, Bob Jones, tell of a lady who trained her pet parrot to say "Good night" and "Good morning." Each evening she would place a cloth covering over the parrot's cage and say, "Good night, Polly," and the parrot would respond, "Good night." In the morning as she lifted the cover off the cage she would say, "Good morning, Polly," and the parrot would say, "Good morning."

One day the parrot escaped from his cage momentarily, and before it was discovered he got into a fight with the family cat. That night when his mistress covered his cage and said, "Good night, Polly," he immediately replied with the usual "Good night." However, when she lifted the cloth from the cage the following day and said, "Good morning, Polly," the parrot replied, "Good night." Shocked at his mistake, she replied again, "Good morning, Polly," only to have him reply the second time, "Good night." Closer examination revealed the parrot's eyes had been scratched out the day before in the fight with the cat and Polly would never again know "Good morning"—only "Good night."

Hell is an eternal "Good night" for every sinner who leaves this life without Christ. Never again will he have a "Good morning" since the sun never rises in that land of anguish and despair. What a terrible thing it is to be lost! [67]

In my first pastorate I preached from Jude 13 about "the blackness of darkness forever," showing the congregation the awfulness of being lost and separated from God forever. An elderly lady visited our service that night. God spoke to her about her lost condition, and she was frightened. She told the friend who had brought her to the service, "I'll never go back to that church. I don't want to hear about that awful place of darkness again."

Her friend said to her, "He'll probably never preach from that verse again," and persuaded the lady to come one more time to our church. I knew nothing about how the sermon had affected her until later. The next time she attended, I once again used the term "the blackness of darkness forever." This time the woman was deeply convicted and trusted Jesus Christ as her personal Savior. She became a faithful member of our church.

Though lost people face "the blackness of darkness forever," Jesus promised, "I am the light of the world: he that followeth me shall not walk in darkness, but shall have the light of life" (John 8:12).

We know that Hell has both fire and darkness; how can this be? The best answer I could find is a statement made by Dr. Henry Morris:

> *All of these specifications seem to point to the likelihood . . . that "hell" . . . will be located on some far-distant star. . . . There are, indeed, stars and galaxies that, although "burning," do not give off light in the visible part of the spectrum, so that they consist of both "fire" and "cloudy darkness."* [68]

Q 39. What is Hell like?

A The results of a poll of thousands of Protestant ministers revealed that 35 percent of the American Baptist ministers, 54 percent of the Presbyterian ministers, 58 percent of the Methodist ministers and 60 percent of the Episcopalian ministers did not believe in a literal Hell. They believed that "Hell does not refer to a special location after death, but to the experience of self-estrangement, guilt, and meaninglessness in this life." [69]

A number of years ago Louis Harris and Associates polled ministerial students at eight leading theological schools in America.

The poll revealed that 71 percent of the students do not believe in a literal Heaven or Hell.[70]

Church historian Martin Marty said, "I have no doubt that the passing of Hell from modern consciousness . . . is one of the major if still largely undocumented modern trends."[71]

A 1983 poll of U.S. Catholics revealed that only one percent pictured Hell as a possible destination for them.

An editorial in a major newspaper asked for more preaching on Hell. Dr. A. C. Dixon said, "If we had more preaching of Hell in the pulpit, we might have less Hell in the community."[72]

Fred Carl Kuehner in "Heaven or Hell?" came to the following conclusions:

> *Today's generation needs to be told what the New Testament teaches about hell and the awful reality of eternal punishment. . . . Coupled with the message of judgment must be the glorious offer of eternal life through faith in the redeeming work of Christ. We must call men to repentance, off the path that leads to hell, and on the way that leads to life everlasting.*[73]

The English word "hell," found fifty-four times in the Bible, is located in the following references:

OLD TESTAMENT

Deuteronomy 32:22	2 Samuel 22:6	Job 11:18	Job 26:6
Psalm 9:17	Psalm 16:10	Psalm 18:5	Psalm 55:15
Psalm 86:13	Psalm 116:3	Psalm 139:8	Proverbs 5:5
Proverbs 7:27	Proverbs 9:18	Proverbs 15:11	Proverbs 15:24
Proverbs 23:14	Proverbs 27:20	Isaiah 5:14	Isaiah 14:9
Isaiah 14:15	Isaiah 28:15	Isaiah 28:18	Isaiah 57:9
Ezekiel 31:16	Ezekiel 31:17	Ezekiel 32:21	Ezekiel 32:27
Amos 9:2	Jonah 2:2	Habakkuk 2:5	

NEW TESTAMENT

Matthew 5:22	Matthew 5:29	Matthew 5:30	Matthew 10:28
Matthew 11:23	Matthew 16:18	Matthew 18:9	Matthew 23:15
Matthew 23:33	Mark 9:43	Mark 9:45	Mark 9:47
Luke 10:15	Luke 12:5	Luke 16:23	Acts 2:27
Acts 2:31	James 3:6	2 Peter 2:4	Revelation 1:18
Revelation 6:8	Revelation 20:13	Revelation 20:14	

HELL FROM A TO Z

Hell will be a place of

A—ABIDING WRATH

"He that believeth on the Son hath everlasting life: and he that believeth not the Son shall not see life; but the wrath of God abideth on him" (John 3:36). This verse says that the wrath of God abides on the sinner right now and that if he dies unsaved, God's wrath will abide on him forever.

Because Jesus Christ suffered the wrath of God against sin at Calvary, we have God's gracious promise that when we trust Him as our personal Lord and Savior, "Much more then, being now justified by his blood, we shall be saved from wrath through him" (Rom. 5:9).

B—BLACKNESS OF DARKNESS FOREVER

"Raging waves of the sea, foaming out their own shame; wandering stars, to whom is reserved the blackness of darkness for ever" (Jude 13).

First Samuel 2:9 tells us that "the wicked shall be silent in darkness." Their condition will so stun and dumbfound them that they will be speechless. Psalm 49:19 says that "they shall never see light." And Peter described the wicked as those "to whom the mist of darkness is reserved for ever" (2 Pet. 2:17).

Though the lost will live with "the blackness of darkness for ever," Jesus said, "I am the light of the world: he that followeth me shall not walk in darkness, but shall have the light of life" (John 8:12).

C—CRYING

At least five times in the New Testament Jesus spoke of the weeping and gnashing of teeth by those in outer darkness (Matt. 8:12; 22:13; 24:51; 25:30; Luke 13:28). Luke 16:24 records that the rich man in Hell "cried."

D—DAMNATION

"But he that shall blaspheme against the Holy Ghost hath never forgiveness, but is in danger of eternal damnation" (Mark 3:29). Jesus asked the question, "How can ye escape the damnation of hell?" (Matt. 23:33). The Bible answers that question: "He that believeth and is baptized shall be saved; but he that believeth not shall be damned" (Mark 16:16). It tells what will happen to those who escape damnation and to those who do not: "And shall come forth; they that have done good, unto the resurrection of life; and they that have done evil, unto the resurrection of damnation" (John 5:29).

Paul spoke of those who refused the truth and were not saved; he wrote concerning them, "That they all might be damned who believed not the truth, but had pleasure in unrighteousness" (2 Thess. 2:12).

E—EVERLASTING PUNISHMENT

"And these shall go away into everlasting punishment: but the righteous into life eternal" (Matt. 25:46).

I have studied the word *aionios,* which means "eternal" or "everlasting," in detail and can prove that this word refers to the punishment of the wicked as being eternal or everlasting.

F—FILTHINESS

"He that is unjust, let him be unjust still: and he which is filthy, let him be filthy still: . . . and he that is holy, let him be holy still" (Rev. 22:11).

God looked down from Heaven to see if any man understood. This is what He saw: "They are all gone aside, they are all together become filthy: there is none that doeth good, no not one" (Ps. 14:2, 3). Job spoke of man and asked, "How much more abominable and filthy is man, which drinketh iniquity like water?" (Job 15:16). And Isaiah wrote concerning man, "But we are all as an unclean thing, and all our righteousnesses are as filthy rags" (Isa. 64:6). The Bible says that people are filthy in this life. If they die unsaved, they will go to a place of filthiness forever.

G—GLOOM

The word "gloom" means "a partial or total darkness; a dark place; an atmosphere of despondency."

Nahum described the goodness of the Lord to those who trust Him, but then He told what will happen to those who do not trust Him: "Darkness shall pursue his [God's] enemies" (Nah. 1:7, 8). In speaking of the wicked, God said, "Wherefore their way shall be unto them as slippery ways in the darkness: they shall be driven on and fall therein" (Jer. 23:12).

Someone wrote the following description of a lost soul's gloom:

Lost amid outer darkness! Lost in the smoke of torment! Lost in the lake of fire and brimstone! Lost amid the howlings of myriads of tormenting devils, the shrieks of the damned, and horrible tempest, the thousand thunders! Lost! Lost!! Lost!!! The bells of eternity are tolling the requiem. Time warned you. The Bible warned you. The Judgment and providences of God warned you. The Spirit warned you. Shall you and your loved ones be lost? Decide now while Jesus calls, or you are lost.[74]

H—HOPELESSNESS

The Bible declares, "When a wicked man dieth, his expectation shall perish: and the hope of unjust men perisheth" (Prov. 11:7), and "The hope of the righteous shall be gladness: but the expectation of the wicked shall perish" (Prov. 10:28). Proverbs 14:32 says just about the same thing: "The wicked is driven away in his wickedness: but the righteous hath hope in his death."

I—INDIGNATION

Indignation is "anger aroused by something unjust, unworthy or mean." God's Word clearly states that God's indignation will come upon the wicked. "But unto them that are contentious, and do not obey the truth, but obey unrighteousness, indignation and wrath, tribulation and anguish, upon every soul of man that doeth evil, of the Jew first, and also of the Gentile" (Rom. 2:8, 9).

"But the LORD is the true God, he is the living God, and an everlasting king: at his wrath the earth shall tremble, and the nations shall not be able to abide his indignation" (Jer. 10:10).

J—JUDGMENT

God has also clearly stated in His Word that a time of judgment is coming. The following verses are some examples: "Rejoice, O young man, in thy youth; and let thy heart cheer thee in the days of thy youth, and walk in the ways of thine heart, and in the sight of thine eyes: but know thou, that for all these things God will bring thee into judgment" (Eccles. 11:9). "For God shall bring every work into judgment, with every secret thing, whether it be good, or whether it be evil" (Eccles. 12:14).

"Because he hath appointed a day, in the which he will judge the world in righteousness by that man whom he hath ordained; whereof he hath given assurance unto all men, in that he hath raised him from the dead" (Acts 17:31). "And as it is appointed unto men once to die, but after this the judgment" (Heb. 9:27).

K—KEEPING

Hell is a place of keeping, where the wicked will be kept for all eternity.

L—LAKE OF FIRE

The Bible mentions the Lake of Fire five times, all in the book of Revelation (19:20; 20:10, 14, 15; 21:8).

Robert G. Gromacki wrote concerning the Lake of Fire:

Actually, there is no good reason to deny the literalness of the lake of fire. If real, resurrected human bodies will go into a real heaven, then a real Satan, real fallen angels, and real bodies of the lost will go into a real place, called the lake of fire.

How can a human body live in a sea of fire without being consumed in a few minutes? The natural bodies we now inhabit could not survive, but remember the unsaved are going to receive new bodies. They will not be glorified bodies, fashioned to the image of Jesus Christ, but they will be of such a composition that they will be able to endure forever the fiery torments without being destroyed. God preserved the three Hebrew children in the midst of Nebuchadnezzar's furnace (Dan. 3). The intermediate body of the rich man did not perish in the torment of hell (Luke 16). So it will be in the lake of fire. God will match the fire with the resurrected body of the unsaved.[75]

M—MEMORY

Hell is a place of memory. Abraham told the rich man in Hell, "Son, remember" (Luke 16:25). In commenting on that man, Dr. G. Beauchamp Vick, late pastor of the Temple Baptist Church in Detroit, Michigan, wrote:

Remember every Gospel message which God let you hear, and yet you said "no" to it all.

Remember every personal worker who pled with you to receive the Lord Jesus Christ and repent of your sins, but you said "no" to it all.

Remember every prayer of a godly Christian mother.

Remember every prayer of all your friends which you ignored.

Yes, my friends, some of you will remember every invitation hymn which you rejected.

You will remember every Gospel invitation to which you said, "no."

You will remember time after time when you sat as the claims of Jesus Christ were being pressed home upon your soul and you hardened your heart, you stiffened your neck and you said, "no" to it all.[76]

N—NO REST

"The same shall drink of the wine of the wrath of God, which is poured out without mixture into the cup of his indignation; and he shall be tormented with fire and brimstone in the presence of the holy angels, and in the presence of the Lamb: And the smoke of their torment ascendeth up for ever and ever: and they have no rest day nor night, who worship the beast and his image, and whosoever receiveth the mark of his name" (Rev. 14:10, 11).

O—OBLIVION

Oblivion means "the condition or state of being blotted out from the memory, forgotten or unknown." Many times I have been asked the question: "How can anyone be happy in Heaven when some of his loved ones are in Hell?" The Bible teaches not only that "the righteous shall be in everlasting remembrance" (Ps. 112:6), but also that those who go to Hell will be forgotten by their loved ones in Heaven. "Drought and heat consume the snow waters: so doth the grave those which have sinned. The womb shall forget him; the worm shall feed sweetly on him; he shall be no more remembered; and wickedness shall be broken as a tree" (Job 24:19, 20).

P—PAIN

Four times in the story of the rich man in Hell we are told of the torment he suffered: "And in hell he lift up his eyes, being in torments. . . . ; I am tormented in this flame. . . . Thou art tormented. . . . this place of torment" (Luke 16:23–25, 28). In Revelation 14:11 we read, "And the smoke of their torment ascendeth up for ever and ever. . . . " People in Hell will have no respite from pain. It will last day and night, forever and ever.

Q—QUANDARY

Quandary means "a state of difficulty, perplexity, uncertainty or hesitation; a predicament." Surely Hell will be all of this and more. "The sinners in Zion are afraid; fearfulness hath surprised the hypocrites. Who among us shall dwell with the devouring fire? who among us shall dwell with everlasting burnings?" (Isa. 33:14). Here God's Word refers to those who "dwell with the devouring fire . . . with everlasting burning."

R—RETRIBUTION

Hell is a place of retribution where God will give to every unsaved person exactly what he deserves. The apostle Paul wrote, "But he that doeth wrong shall receive for the wrong which he hath done: and there is no respect of persons" (Col. 3:25).

S—SHAME

In speaking of the Resurrection, the Bible says: "And many of them that sleep in the dust of the earth shall awake, some to everlasting life, and some to shame and everlasting contempt" (Dan. 12:2). In other words, the unsaved will awake to shame and everlasting contempt.

T—THIRST

The rich man in Hell begged for water. "And he cried and said, Father Abraham, have mercy on me, and send Lazarus, that he may dip the tip of his finger in water, and cool my tongue; for I am tormented in this flame" (Luke 16:24). He wanted even one drop of water.

U—UNGODLINESS

The ungodly in this world will go to a place of ungodliness in the next world. The question was asked, "Where shall the ungodly and the sinner appear?" (1 Pet. 4:18). The psalmist answered, "The ungodly are not so, but are like the chaff which the wind driveth away" and "the way of the ungodly shall perish" (Ps. 1:4, 6).

V—VENGEANCE

God declared, "To me belongeth vengeance, and recompense; their foot shall slide in due time: for the day of their calamity is at hand, and the things that shall come upon them make haste" (Deut. 32:35). Jonathan Edwards preached his well-known and greatly used sermon, "Sinners in the Hands of an Angry God" based on this passage of Scripture. His text was "their foot shall slide in due time."

W—WOE

God's Word pronounces a woe unto the wicked: "Woe unto the wicked! it shall be ill with him: for the reward of his hands shall be given him" (Isa. 3:11). Jesus said concerning Judas, "Woe unto that man by whom the Son of man is betrayed! it had been good for that man if he had not been born" (Matt. 26:24). As someone has well said, "Better not to have been born at all than not to have been born again." Someone else has said, "Born once, die twice; born twice, die once."

Catherine Dangell has written a stirring poem titled "The Horrors of Hell":

Hell, the prisonhouse of despair,
Here are some things that won't be there:
No flowers will bloom on the banks of Hell,
No beauties of nature we love so well;
No comforts of home, music and song,
No friendship of joy will be found in that throng;
No children to brighten the long, weary night;
No love nor peace, nor one ray of light;
No blood-washed soul with face beaming bright,
No loving smile in that region of night;
No mercy, no pity, pardon nor grace,
No water, Oh, God, what a terrible place:
The pangs of the lost no human can tell,
Not one moment's ease—there is no rest in Hell.

Hell, the prisonhouse of despair,
Here are some things that will be there:
Fire and brimstone are there, we know,
For God in His Word hath told us so:
Memory, remorse, suffering and pain,
Weeping and wailing, but all in vain;
Blasphemer, swearer, hater of God,
Christ-rejecter while here on earth trod;
Murderer, gambler, drunkard and liar,
Will have his part in the lake of fire;
The filthy, the vile, the cruel and mean,
What a horrible mob in Hell will be seen:
Yes, more than humans on earth can tell,
Are torments and woes of Eternal Hell.[77]

X—EXCLUSION

The dictionary gives the meaning of "exclusion" as "the state of being excluded." "Exclude" means "to shut out; to put out." "Excluding" implies keeping out what is already outside. In speaking of the holy city, New Jerusalem, the abode of the saints of God for eternity, God said: "And there shall in no wise enter into it any thing that defileth, neither whatsoever worketh abomination, or maketh a lie: but they which are written in the Lamb's book of life" (Rev. 21:27).

"For without are dogs, and sorcerers, and whoremongers, and murderers, and idolaters, and whosoever loveth and maketh a lie" (Rev. 22:15). This verse clearly teaches that the unsaved will be "without," or outside, the city. They cannot enter that beautiful place but are excluded from it forever.

Y—YEARNING

"Yearn" means "to feel mental uneasiness from longing desire; to be filled with eager longing; to desire; to long for; crave." D. M. Fletcher wrote "Soliloquy of a Lost Soul," which reflects the yearning of a soul in Hell:

At last I am in hell. In spite of all my resolutions not to come, I am
here to suffer the just demands of a broken law. O God, can it be
that I, who was taught the way of truth, virtue and Heaven, should
choose sin and eternal damnation?

66

Oh, that I had a moment in which to repent; but it will never be given. I sealed my doom. God's mercy was extended; I refused till too late. Now Eternal Justice is being satisfied. 'Tis just. God is love; is just and holy. He is clear, but I am guilty—damned, and that righteously.[78]

Z—ZERO EXISTENCE

"Zero" means "figuratively, the lowest point; nothingness; nullity; a person or thing that has no importance, influence, or independent existence." In Hell a person will have "no importance, influence or independent existence." He will be at "the lowest point."

Although God declared that His anger will kindle a fire and will burn unto the lowest Hell (Deut. 32:22), David rejoiced in God's salvation and uttered these words of praise to God: "For great is thy mercy toward me: and thou hast delivered my soul from the lowest hell" (Ps. 86:13). Through repentance toward God and faith toward our Lord Jesus Christ we can be delivered from "zero existence," "the lowest point," and we can go to Heaven and "be the children of the Highest" (Luke 6:35).

Years ago the noted missionary Adoniram Judson spent many days giving out gospel tracts on the borders of Siam (Thailand) and China. Two or three months later he received a letter from one of the distant fields. It read as follows: "Sir, we hear there is an eternal Hell. We are afraid of it. Do give us a writing that tells us how to escape it."

I pray that many readers of this book will be like this man as he spoke of Hell—"afraid of it."

Evangelist Jim Mercer said, "It is better to be Hell-scared then Hell-scarred."[79]

T. DeWitt Talmadge stated: "I believe there is a hell. If I had not been afraid of hell, I do not think I should have started for heaven."[80]

Jesus Christ spoke pointedly to some people in His day: "Ye serpents, ye generation of vipers, how can ye escape the damnation of hell?" (Matt. 23:33).

René Pache wrote, "To be lost, man need do nothing; he is a sinner, condemned by the law of God; and he need simply stay as he is to go directly to hell."[81]

God's Word is plain. In order to escape the damnation of Hell,

- a person must repent;
- a person must believe on the Lord Jesus Christ.

Jesus Christ made it clear that if people do not repent, they will perish or go to Hell: "I tell you, Nay: but, except ye repent, ye shall all likewise perish" (Luke 13:3). He commanded in Mark 1:15: "Repent ye, and believe the gospel." Paul preached "repentance toward God, and faith toward our Lord Jesus Christ" (Acts 20:21).

"Repentance" means "to change the mind" or "to have another mind," and it involves both a turning from sin and a turning to God. It touches the intellect, the emotions and the will.

Emory Bancroft wrote about repentance and faith: "In repentance, the sinner turns away from sin; in faith he turns to Christ. These are inseparable. . . . True repentance cannot exist apart from faith, nor faith, from repentance."[82]

Every sinner is dead in trespasses and sins and cannot and will not repent and believe on Christ on his own. God, in His amazing grace, draws all men and gives the sinner the ability to repent, believe on Christ and be saved. After a person is saved, he can look back on his life and realize that his salvation is completely by God's grace. On the other hand, if a person dies in his sins, in Hell he must look back and say, "I refused to come to Christ, so I have only myself to blame. I deserve Hell."

God is "not willing that any should perish, but that all should come to repentance" (2 Pet. 3:9). John 3:16 states: "For God so loved the world, that he gave his only begotten Son, that whosoever believeth in him should not perish, but have everlasting life." In these two verses God promises that those who repent and believe on the Lord Jesus Christ will not perish (or go to Hell). Come to God today in repentance and faith—there is danger in delay.

Q 40. Will there be degrees of punishment in Hell?

A Early in my ministry I heard a pastor tell his congregation that everybody will get the same reward in Heaven. He misinterpreted the teaching of Jesus in His parable of the laborers in Matthew 20:1–16. Later in my ministry I taught a class at a Bible institute. As I taught the students that Hell will have different degrees of punishment, a student responded, "I don't believe that."

At the close of the Millennium, all unsaved people from the first one to the last one will stand before the Great White Throne Judgment (Rev. 20:11–15). Billions of sinners will be there. Jesus Christ will be the Judge, for He said, "For the Father judgeth no man, but hath committed all judgment unto the Son" (John 5:22; see also John 5:27; Acts 10:42; 17:31; Rom. 2:16).

Hebrews 9:27 informs us about the two most important appointments we must keep: "And as it is appointed unto men once to die, but after this the judgment." When Jesus Christ judges the unsaved, His judgment will be according to the following criteria:

- truth (Rom. 2:2);
- accumulated guilt (Rom. 2:5);
- deeds (Rom. 2:6; see also Job 34:11; Ps. 62:12; Prov. 12:14; 24:12; Isa. 3:11; 59:18; Jer. 32:19; Ezek. 7:3, 27; Hos. 4:9; Rev. 20:11–15);
- impartiality (Rom. 2:11);
- secrets of the heart (Rom. 2:16; see also Eccles. 12:14);
- the gospel (Rom. 2:16);
- the Word of God (John 12:48);
- righteousness (Ps. 9:7, 8; see also Ps. 96:13).

In three places in the New Testament Jesus said some would receive "greater damnation" (Matt. 23:14; Mark 12:40; Luke 20:47). Six times in the New Testament we have the words of Jesus Christ as He warned the people in Chorazin, Bethsaida and Capernaum that it will be "more tolerable" at the judgment for the wicked cities of Sodom and Gomorrha and Tyre and Sidon than it will be for them (Matt. 10:15; 11:22, 24; Mark 6:11; Luke 10:12, 14). Jesus also said, "And that servant, which knew his lord's will, and prepared not himself, neither did according to his will, shall be beaten with many stripes. But he that knew not, and did commit things worthy of stripes, shall be beaten with few stripes. For unto whomsoever much is given, of him shall be much required: and to whom men have committed much, of him they will ask the more" (Luke 12:47, 48). Dr. James A. Borland commented on these two verses: "The fact that there will be degrees of punishment is taught here. The torment of hell will not be uniformly felt. The light one possesses helps determine how responsible one is. Some will be found more guilty than others, but no lost man can claim innocency in that day."[83]

In his helpful commentary on Luke, J. C. Ryle wrote:

Let us observe, lastly, in this passage, that there will be degrees of condemnation and misery in hell. *The words of our Lord are distinct and express. He says of those who live and die hypocrites, "the same shall receive greater damnation."*

The subject opened up in these words is a deeply painful one. The reality and eternity of future punishment are among the great foundation truths of revealed religion, which it is hard to think upon without a shudder. But it is well to have all that the Bible teaches about heaven and hell firmly fixed on our minds. The Bible teaches distinctly that there will be degrees of glory in heaven. It teaches with no less distinctness, both here and elsewhere, that there will be degrees of misery in hell.

Who, after all, are those who will finally receive condemnation? This is the practical point that concerns us most. All who will not come to Christ—all who know not God and obey not the Gospel— all who refuse to repent, and go on still in wickedness, all such will be finally condemned. They will reap according as they have sown. God willeth not their eternal ruin. But if they will not hear His voice, they must die in their sins.

But who . . . will receive the heaviest condemnation? It will not fall on heathens who never heard the truth. It will not fall on ignorant and neglected Englishmen, for whose souls, however sunk in profligacy, no man cared. It will fall on those who had great light and knowledge, but made no proper use of it. It will fall on those who professed great sanctity and religiousness, but in reality clung to their sins. In one word, the hypocrite will have the lowest place in hell. These are awful things. But they are true.[84]

Q
41. Will people be together or isolated in the Lake of Fire?

A
Through the years I have heard many people jokingly say, "If I go to Hell, at least I'll be with my friends." Irving S. Cobb, internationally famous humorist and writer, wrote, "Hell may have a worse climate but undoubtedly the company is sprightlier."[85] Some people think that those in Hell will see others there, talk with them and even have a great time together. But the Bible describes those who go to Hell and compares them to ". . . wandering stars, to whom is reserved the blackness of darkness for ever" (Jude 13). Wandering stars, like "shooting" stars, "move across the sky, shining briefly, and then vanish without producing light or giving direction. . . . Similarly, the prominence of apostate leaders is short-lived, useless and false."[86] These wandering stars just keep going around and around so far from any other star that they never meet another star. Think of a lost soul, totally alone, just wandering forever.

God's Word says in 1 Samuel 2:9: ". . . the wicked shall be silent in darkness." Those who go to Hell will be dumbfounded and speechless; they will not talk to others. They will use their mouths and voices to make sounds like groans and will weep, wail and gnash their teeth.

The lost will have no use for their eyes either. Referring to the unsaved, God declared ". . . they shall never see light" (Ps. 49:19). Hell will be in perpetual darkness throughout eternity. "He shall be driven from light into darkness, and chased out of the world. . . . Surely such are the dwellings of the wicked, and this is the place of him that knoweth not God" (Job 18:18, 21).

The parable of the marriage feast in Matthew 22:1–14 reinforces the ideas of speechlessness and darkness in Hell. The man who did not have a wedding garment (an unsaved person) could not speak. "Then said the king to the servants, Bind him hand and foot, and take him away, and cast him into outer darkness; there shall be weeping and gnashing of teeth" (v. 13).

George H. Mundell, in his stirring booklet, *Destiny of a Lost Soul*, commented,

The fact of darkness is repeated, but beyond that there is the binding of the hands and feet. . . .

Some people to whom I have spoken about a lost eternity have said, "Oh, well, I'll spend probably the first ten thousand years just shaking hands with all my friends who have gone there." Oh, how unwise! I thank God for showing us this fact. There will be no use of the hands, no shaking of hands. Besides, the souls in a lost eternity will be so far apart that they will never see or know that there is anyone else there.

The binding of the feet means that the person may no longer go and come as he pleases. He stays right where he is.

Just think: there will be no use for eyes, since there will be nothing to see. There will be no use for the lips, for there will be no one to talk with. The mouth will be used only for groaning and weeping and gnashing of teeth. There will be no use for hands, for there will be nothing to do. There will be no use for feet, for the lost soul will not have freedom of movement.[87]

What to do to escape Hell and go to Heaven is easy. Acts 16:31 says, "Believe on the Lord Jesus Christ, and thou shalt be saved." Simply believe that Jesus Christ, God's perfect and holy Son, shed His blood on the cross to take our punishment and to make us right with God. He paid for every sin that you and I have committed or will commit. All we have to do is accept His gift of salvation. Romans 10:13 declares, "For whosoever [that includes you] shall call upon the name of the Lord shall be saved." Will you believe on Him today, accept His gift of eternal life and flee Hell to live in Heaven forever with Him?

Q 42. Even though Heaven will be filled with great happiness after the Rapture, how will God comfort us about loved ones who are not there?

A Years ago in a gospel service the speaker said, "I have learned that if you are saved, I will know you when we get to Heaven, but if you're not saved, I will not miss you." I have never forgotten that statement. What a blessed time we will have in seeing our loved ones and friends and fellowshipping with them throughout eternity. But those who rejected the Lord Jesus Christ will not be there, and we will not miss them. God's Word says, "The righteous shall be in everlasting remembrance" (Ps. 112:6). But the lost will be forever forgotten: "Drought and heat consume the snow waters: so doth the grave [sheol] those which have sinned. The womb [the mother] shall forget him; . . . he [the sinner] shall be no more remembered . . . " (Job 24:19, 20). What a terrible thought—that even your own mother will forget you and no one will ever remember you! "Forgotten by a mother's womb! Deserted even of the most tenacious affections the human heart can know, worms make a dainty repast upon his flesh."[88] "The wicked shall be turned into hell, and all the nations that forget God" (Ps. 9:17). Those who have forgotten God will be forgotten by those who dwell with Him. God promised: "For, behold, I create new heavens and a new earth: and the former shall not be remembered, nor come into mind" (Isa. 65:17). So here is God's answer to the question of how a person can be happy in Heaven when some of his loved ones are in Hell: Those in Heaven will not even remember those who are not there. They will forget the lost forever.

Q 43. Will we know one another in Heaven?

A Time and time again I have had people ask me this question. One person said, "If I could be sure of a hereafter and know that I should meet the loved ones gone before, I would crawl on my hands and knees from New York to San Francisco, just to gain that knowledge."

The Welsh preacher, John Evans, was asked one day by his wife,

"John, I have been thinking and wondering how it will be in heaven. Do you really believe that we shall know each other there?"

"Why, my dear," replied Evans, "do you think we shall be bigger fools there than we are here? We know each other here. Shall we not know each other there? To be sure we shall."[89]

Dr. John Dick, in his *Lectures on Theology* said,

One should think that the question was unnecessary, as the answer naturally presents itself to every man's mind. . . . What reason can be given why they should not? . . . What would be gained by this ignorance no man can tell; but we can tell what would be lost by it. They would lose all the happiness of meeting again on the peaceful shore, those from whom they were separated by the storms of life; of seeing among the trophies of Divine grace, many of whom they had despaired, and for whose sake they had gone down with sorrow to the grave; of knowing the good which they had been honored to do, and being surrounded with the individuals who had been saved by means of their prayers, and instructions, and labors.[90]

Paul wrote in 1 Corinthians 13:12: "For now we see through a glass, darkly; but then face to face: now I know in part; but then shall I know even as also I am known." In Paul's day a glass (mirror) was made of brass, which means it was not as bright and distinct as our modern glass mirrors. Paul meant that our present knowledge is like the indistinct image of a brass mirror, but our future knowledge will be distinct and clear. Then we shall fully know, even as God fully knows us now.

Before we can recognize our loved ones in Heaven, both we and they must be there. By the grace of God I'll be there. Will you? The Lord Jesus Christ pointed out the way to Heaven when He said, "I am the way, the truth, and the life: no man cometh unto the Father, but by me" (John 14:6).

Dr. William E. Bierderwolf, an evangelist used of God in years past, related the story of an earnest Christian engineer who looked forward to a blessed recognition and reunion in Heaven:

Some years ago, every night as I neared the end of my run, I would look up to the top of a hill where stood a little cottage. . . . I would pull open the whistle and let out a blast and then an old lady would come out . . . and wave her hand at me. And as we shot into the tunnel she would go into the house and say, "Thank God, father, Bennie is safe home tonight!" But the day came when we carried mother out and laid her to rest. Then night after night when I pulled the whistle, an old man would come to the door and wave his hand to me, and I could almost hear him say as he entered the house, "Thank God, Bennie is safe home tonight!" But now they are both gone. . . . But some day when I have pulled the whistle for the last time and the work of this world is over, I shall come to the ... gates and I am sure as I draw near, I shall see an old lady waiting at the entrance alongside an old gentleman, and as I enter I shall see my dear old mother turn to father and say, "Thank God, father, Bennie is safe home at last!"[91]

Q 44. Is Heaven getting full with the millions of babies killed by abortion?

A It is a fact that millions of babies are killed in abortions. These statistics were given in a recent book concerning abortions.

WORLDWIDE	IN AMERICA
(55 million are killed every year.)	(1.6 million are killed every year.)
150,685 every day	4,383 every day
6,278 every hour	183 every hour
105 every minute	3 every minute

More than 25 million babies have been aborted in America since 1973, when the Supreme Court decided *Roe* v. *Wade*. These millions of aborted babies are real people who will live forever in Heaven. Jesus Christ's death on the cross made provision for the salvation of all people (2 Cor. 5:19; 1 John 2:2). All, including infants, are rendered savable through the Atonement. Dr. Robert Gromacki taught the following beliefs concerning infants:

God is the One who gives life and the One who takes away life (see Job 1:21). He determines the life span of each human. If He chooses to take the life of a child before that child has the capacity to believe or to reject, then that prerogative expresses His divine will and pleasure.

Salvation is completely of God, who has mercy on whom He wills (see Rom. 9:15, 16, 18). If He chooses to save one who is unable to believe, then that action will glorify Him and will manifest His sovereign, gracious counsel.

Thus, the sense of Scripture seems to indicate that all infants who die before the indeterminate age of accountability enter immediately into the eternal presence of God. This truth equally applies to those with severe mental retardation.[92]

In his tract "Human Life before Birth," Dean Dan Lyons quoted the following report from an article in *Life* magazine. "The birth of a human life really occurs at the moment the mother's egg cell is fertilized by one of the father's sperm cells."[93]

Lyons also quoted *California Medicine,* the official journal of the California Medical Association, which stated in the September 1970 issue, "It is a scientific fact [that] human life begins at conception and is continuous, whether intra- or extra-uterine, until death."[94]

In 1984, 61 physicians (including two past presidents of the American College of Obstetrics and Gynecology) signed a statement titled "The Utmost Respect for Human Life," which reads in part, "We urge all those engaged in the abortion debate to recognize that a central issue in the discourse must include acceptance of the fact that induced abortion causes the death of a living human" *(emphasis added).[95]*

"Physicians, biologists, and other scientists agree that conception . . . marks the beginning of the life of a human being—a being that is alive and is a member of the human species. There is overwhelming agreement on this point in countless medical, biological, and scientific writings."[96]

Professor M. Matthews Roth of Harvard University wrote, "It is scientifically correct to say that individual human life begins at conception."[97]

Professor H. Gordon of Mayo Clinic wrote, "It is an established fact that human life begins at conception."[98]

Dr. Henry Morris wrote the following statements concerning the issue:

There is every reason to believe, therefore, and no reason to doubt, that each individual becomes a whole person—body, soul, and spirit—at the very moment of his conception. Whether or not he survives through childhood, or even survives to birth, he has an eternal spirit which will live forever.[99]

What a tragedy that every year in the world about 55 million babies are killed by abortion, but what a blessing to know that 55 million babies go immediately to Heaven and will be there forever and ever. "Where sin abounded, grace did much more abound" (Rom. 5:20).

Heaven is not even close to being full, for it has unlimited room for all who desire to go there. Jesus Christ is the Way (John 14:6).

Q 45. If Heaven is enormously big, how could it land on earth?

A At the close of the Millennium, the first heaven and the first earth will pass away; but God promises "For, behold, I create new heavens and a new earth" (Isa. 65:17). We are told, "there was no more sea" (Rev. 21:1; cf. 2 Pet. 3:10–13). Today about three-fourths of the surface of the earth is water, and more than half of the land surface is uninhabitable. Geological changes will take place in the earth so that the new earth will have more than eight times as much space for habitation as the present earth has.

Not only will there be a new heaven and a new earth in the future, but there will also be a new city called "the holy city, New Jerusalem" (Rev. 21:2). According to this verse, John saw this city "coming down from God out of heaven." It is not Heaven, for it will come down from God out of Heaven. It will take up its abode on the new earth and will be the dwelling place for all eternity for God's people. In chapter 12, verses 22 to 24, the writer of Hebrews named the inhabitants of that new city:

> But ye are come unto Mount Sion, and unto the city of the living God, the heavenly Jerusalem, and to an innumerable company of angels, to the general assembly and church of the firstborn, which are written in heaven, and to God the Judge of all, and to the spirits of just men made perfect, and to Jesus the mediator of the new covenant, and to the blood of sprinkling, that speaketh better things than that of Abel.

Notice the inhabitants of the city: an innumerable company of angels; church saints, saved in this age of grace; God; spirits of just men made perfect (the Old Testament saints) and Jesus.

Revelation 21:10–21 gives the dimensions of the city: it will be 1,500 miles long, 1,500 miles wide and 1,500 miles high.

Q 46. When someone gets saved right before he dies, where will he go?

A The person who gets saved right before he dies goes immediately to Paradise, which is now in the third heaven (2 Cor. 12:2–4). Before Christ's resurrection and ascension, Paradise was located in the heart of the earth (cf. Matt. 12:40; Acts 2:27, 31; Luke 16:19–31; 23:39–43), and the saved ones of the Old Testament went there at death and were comforted (Luke 16:25). When Christ ascended, He led out those in Paradise and took them to the third heaven, where the saved ones of the New Testament went at death (Eph. 4:8–10).

The thief on the cross trusted Christ as his Savior while he was dying on the cross, and Jesus promised him, "Verily I say unto thee, To day shalt thou be with me in paradise" (Luke 23:43). At death, the saved person is " . . . absent from the body [and] . . . present with the Lord" (2 Cor. 5:8).

I would not encourage anyone to wait until right before he dies to trust Christ as his Savior. Someone has said, "The person who plans to get saved at the eleventh hour usually dies at ten-thirty." The Bible tells us, "Now is the accepted time; behold, now is the day of salvation" (2 Cor. 6:2).

Dr. C. I. Scofield commented on the two thieves crucified with Christ: "One thief was saved, that none need despair; but only one, that none should presume."[100]

78

Q 47. What is Heaven like?

A Of all the questions people have asked me, this one has been asked the most. Children, teenagers and adults have asked about Heaven.

A class of third-graders from a school in Union City, Tennessee, was asked, "What is Heaven like?" A little boy diplomatically wrote: "Heaven is where some very nice teachers and a nice principal will be found." Another child wrote: "Heaven is where you will get everything you want, but if you want too much you might not go there." But the answer that I liked the best was given by a little girl: "Heaven should be the happiest part of my dead life."

Someone has recorded the following incident in the life of Pepper Martin, the hero of the St. Louis Cardinals in the 1931 World Series.

When Pepper Martin . . . was asked, "What is your ambition?" he answered: "My ambition is to go to heaven!"

When his flippant questioner guffawed: "You wanta play a harp, eh?" Pepper Martin knocked a verbal homer by saying, "Mister, I don't think that's funny. . . . I should be used to it by now, but I'm not. People don't want to be mean, I guess, but they sure do pretty well without trying. All I've got to say is this: If there's anything wrong in reading the Bible every day and believing what's in it; if there's anything wrong in a man wanting to go back to the soil and live the plain life of a farmer; if there's anything wrong in raising vegetables and loving animals; if there's anything funny about wanting to go to heaven when you die—then I'm afraid that life isn't worth living."[101]

The word "heaven" is found in the Bible about 550 times, and the word has three different meanings. Most uses of the word "heaven" have to do with the first and second heavens.

The first heaven is the region of the clouds, or the atmospheric heavens, immediately above us. The space known as the troposphere extends to about 10 miles above the earth. The stratosphere extends from 20 to 30 miles beyond that. The mesosphere is the space from 30 to 50 miles above the stratosphere. The ionosphere ranges up to 300 miles beyond the mesosphere, and then the exosphere begins. It extends to at least 600 miles above the earth and then gradually fades into outer space.[102] (See Genesis 1:20; 7:11 and Acts 14:17.)

The second heaven is the celestial heavens (outer space), the sphere in which the sun, moon and stars appear. (See Psalms 8:3 and 19:1.)

The third Heaven, the highest Heaven, is God's abode. (See Matthew 6:9; 2 Cor. 12:1–4 and Revelation 11:13.) Heaven, the abode of God, is in the north. In recounting the fall of Satan, Isaiah gives us an idea about the location of Heaven:

How art thou fallen from heaven, O Lucifer, son of the morning! How art thou cut down to the ground, which didst weaken the nations! For thou hast said in thine heart, I will ascend into heaven, I will exalt my throne above the stars of God: I will sit also upon the mount of the congregation, in the sides of the north: I will ascend above the heights of the clouds; I will be like the most High (Isa. 14:12–14).

This passage of Scripture tells us that Heaven is above the stars of God, in the sides of the north and above the heights of the clouds. North is in the same direction from every point on the universe. Job 26:7 says, "He stretcheth out the north over the empty place, and hangeth the earth upon nothing."

Modern astronomers tell us that in the north, in the constellation of the Swan, there is a rift in the heavens, a place where no stars exist. The great telescopes of Yerkes Observatory located at Williams Bay, Wisconsin, and at Mount Palomar, California, have taken photographs of this rift. The photographs show us that an empty place, such as Job described, does exist. The astronomers also tell us that the earth is moving toward this empty place hour by hour, day by day, month by month and year after year at the tremendous speed of 600 miles per minute.[103]

Psalm 75:6 and 7 also refer to Heaven: "For promotion cometh neither from the east, nor from the west, nor from the south. But God is the judge: he putteth down one, and setteth up another." The throne of God, the place where God judges, is located, not in the east, west or south, but in the north.

The Bible likens Heaven to
- a building (John 14:2);
- a temple (Rev. 21:22);
- a city (Heb. 11:10, 16; 12:22; 13:14; Rev. 21:2, 10, 16, 21, 23; 22:14);
- a country (Heb. 11:16);
- an inheritance (Acts 20:32; Col. 1:12; Heb. 11:16; 1 Pet. 1:4).

When God's people die, they go to live with the Lord in Heaven, the third Heaven, where God is (2 Cor. 5:1–8; Phil. 1:21, 23; 1 Thess. 4:13–18).

When Christ returns at the Rapture, the Church saints who have died and are in Heaven will come with Him. They will receive their resurrection bodies. The living believers will "be changed, in a moment, in the twinkling of an eye" (1 Cor. 15:51, 52). Then we all will go to the Judgment Seat of Christ to have our works tested.

At the close of the tribulation period, God will resurrect the Old Testament believers and the saints who have been martyred in the tribulation period (Dan. 12:1, 2; Rev. 20:4). Christ will then reign on the earth for 1,000 years. At the close of the Millennium, God will burn up this earth, but He will then create a new earth (Isa. 65:17; 2 Pet. 3:10–13; Rev. 21:1). The Bible also provides us with the following information:

And I John saw the holy city, new Jerusalem, coming down from God out of heaven, prepared as a bride adorned for her husband. And I heard a great voice out of heaven saying, Behold, the tabernacle of God is with men, and he will dwell with them, and they shall be his people, and God himself shall be with them, and be their God. And God shall wipe away all tears from their eyes; and there shall be no more death, neither sorrow, nor crying, neither shall there be any more pain: for the former things are passed away (Rev. 21:2–4).

Notice that the holy city, New Jerusalem, will come down from God out of Heaven. The holy city is not Heaven, although the New Jerusalem is usually what people refer to when they speak of going to Heaven. This city is the one Abraham looked for (Heb. 11:10), people seek (Heb. 13:14) and God has prepared (Heb. 11:16). According to Hebrews 12:22–24, the people who will live in this beautiful city include the following:

- "an innumerable company of angels";
- "the general assembly and church of the firstborn, which are written in heaven"—the Church saints of this dispensation, those saved from the Day of Pentecost to the Rapture of the Church;
- "God the Judge of all";
- "The spirits of just men made perfect"—the Old Testament saints;
- "Jesus the mediator of the new covenant."

Dr. John F. Walvoord made the following comments on this passage of Scripture:

> *The anticipation of Hebrews 12:22–24 is specifically that the heavenly Jerusalem will include not only God and an innumerable company of angels but also the general assembly and church of the firstborn, that is, the saints of the present age and the spirits of just men made perfect, that is, all other saints.*[104]

This city will be our headquarters for all eternity. It will rest on the new earth that God will create. Dr. Walvoord also wrote, "The new Jerusalem will have the distinction of being the residence of the saints, but it is implied that they will be able to travel elsewhere on the new earth and possibly also in the new heaven."[105]

Revelation 21 describes the new city. It is
- a holy city (v. 2);
- a city having the glory of God (v. 11);
- a city that has light like a precious stone (v. 11);
- a city with a great and high wall (v. 12);
- a city with twelve gates (v. 12);
- a city with twelve foundations (v. 14);
- a city foursquare and 1,500 miles long, wide and high (v. 16);
- a city with a jasper wall (v. 18);
- a city of pure gold, like clear glass (v. 18);
- a city with the foundations of the wall garnished with all manner of precious stones (vv. 19, 20);
- a city with twelve pearl gates (v. 21);
- a city with no temple—"the Lord God Almighty and the Lamb are the temple of it" (v. 22);
- a city that has no need of the sun or moon, for the glory of God and the Lamb is the light of it (v. 23);

- a city in which the nations of those who are saved walk in its light (v. 24);
- a city into which the kings of the earth bring their glory and honor (v. 24);
- a city with open gates (v. 25);
- a city with no night (v. 25);
- a city into which nothing that defiles or works abomination or makes a lie can enter (v. 27);
- a city that allows only those who are written in the Lamb's book of life to enter (v. 27).

People ask, "What will we do in Heaven?" Some people seem to think they will be bored in Heaven.

Someone has told the story of a small boy who had been told that if he went to Heaven, he would sit on a stool and play a golden harp. Of course, he didn't want to do that.

Another story concerns a dying old lady who, although devout, was apprehensive about leaving this world. Those standing by talked to her about Heaven and asked her what she thought it would be like. She replied: "Oh, there must be chairs arranged the way they are in church. People sit on them and sing psalms during all eternity." No wonder she preferred this earth to such a Heaven as that!

What *will* believers do throughout eternity?

They will worship Him. The Bible describes this worship:

And when he had taken the book, the four beasts and four and twenty elders fell down before the Lamb, having every one of them harps, and golden vials full of odours, which are the prayers of saints. And they sung a new song, saying, Thou art worthy to take the book, and to open the seals thereof: for thou wast slain, and hast redeemed us to God by thy blood out of every kindred, and tongue, and people, and nation; and hast made us unto our God kings and priests: and we shall reign on the earth. And I beheld, and I heard the voice of many angels round about the throne and the beasts and the elders: and the number of them was ten thousand times ten thousand, and thousands of thousands; saying with a loud voice, Worthy is the Lamb that was slain to receive power, and riches, and wisdom, and strength, and honour, and glory, and blessing. And every creature which is in heaven, and on the earth, and under the earth, and such as are in the sea, and all that are in them, heard I saying, Blessing, and honour, and glory, and power, be unto him that sitteth upon the throne, and unto the Lamb for ever and ever. And the four beasts said, Amen. And the four and twenty elders fell down and worshipped him that liveth for ever and ever. . . . And I heard as it were the voice of a great multitude, and as the voice of many waters, and as the voice of mighty thunderings, saying, Alleluia: for the Lord God omnipotent reigneth (Rev. 5:8–14; 19:6).

They will serve Him. "And his servants shall serve him" (Rev. 22:3). Forever God's people will serve Him. We will constantly labor for the Lord, yet we will not become weary or fail in our work. Walter Scott wrote: "Ours will be a service without cessation, without weariness, without flagging energy. In joy and freedom our service then will be one of pure love; without a flaw, and without one legal thought. How varied the character of service! How gladly the whole being enters upon an eternal life of service to Him!"[106]

They will see His face. "And they shall see his face" (Rev. 22:4). God told Moses, "Thou canst not see my face: for there shall no man see me, and live. And I will take away mine hand, and thou shalt see my back parts: but my face shall not be seen" (Exod. 33:20, 23). Jesus promised, "Blessed are the pure in heart: for they shall see God" (Matt. 5:8). The psalmist humbly prayed, "As for me, I will behold thy face in righteousness: I shall be satisfied, when I awake, with thy likeness" (Ps. 17:15). As Fanny Crosby wrote, "And I shall see Him face to face, / And tell the story—Saved by grace."

They will have His name in their foreheads. "And his name shall be in their foreheads" (Rev. 22:4). They shall openly and publicly bear His name, signifying that they belong to Him. They are branded forever as His very own.

They will be with Him. Paul, in speaking of the coming of Christ for His own, said that we will "meet the Lord in the air: and so shall we ever be with the Lord" (1 Thess. 4:17). John wrote, "Behold, the tabernacle of God is with men, and he will dwell with them, and they shall be his people, and God himself shall be with them, and be their God" (Rev. 21:3). Jesus promised, "I will come again, and receive you unto myself; that where I am, there ye may be also" (John 14:3); and He prayed, "Father, I will that they also, whom thou hast given me, be with me where I am" (John 17:24). God's people will forever be with Him and His Son to enjoy intimate fellowship for all eternity. God's agelong purpose to dwell with His people will be finally and fully realized.

They will be like Him. God's people have this promise: "Beloved, now are we the sons of God, and it doth not yet appear what we shall be: but we know that, when he shall appear, we shall be like him; for we shall see him as he is" (1 John 3:2). Philippians 3:20 and 21 also make a promise: "For our conversation is in heaven; from whence also we look for the Saviour, the Lord Jesus Christ: Who shall change our vile body, that it may be fashioned like unto his glorious body, according to the working whereby he is able even to subdue all things unto himself." Paul declared in Romans 8:29, "For whom he did foreknow, he also did predestinate to be conformed to the image of his Son."

C. H. Spurgeon had received a copy of *Studies in Leviticus* from its author, Andrew Bonar. Spurgeon wrote to Bonar to ask for the writer's picture and autograph to be placed in the book. Bonar replied, "I will do as you request, but I am sorry you could not wait a while, for I could have sent you a better picture, for I shall be like Him!"[107]

They will reign with Him eternally. "And they shall reign for ever and ever" (Rev. 22:5). After we believers reign with Christ in the Millennium, we will continue to reign with Him throughout eternity. We will never cease to reign with Him. Revelation 11:15 says of Christ: "The kingdoms of this world are become the kingdoms of our Lord, and of his Christ; and he shall reign for ever and ever"; and chapter 22, verse 5, says of His people, " . . . And they shall reign for ever and ever."

Dr. R. G. Lee said in one of his sermons:

In Heaven beauty has reached perfection. Dr. Biederwolf tells us of a little girl who was blind from birth and only knew the beauties of earth from her mother's lips. A noted surgeon worked on her eyes and at last his operations were successful, and as the last bandage dropped away she flew into her mother's arms and then to the window and the open door, and as the glories of earth rolled into her vision, she ran screaming back to her mother and said, "Oh, Mama, why didn't you tell me it was so beautiful?" And the mother wiped her tears of joy away and said, "My precious child, I tried to tell you but I couldn't do it." And one day when we go sweeping through those gates of pearl and catch our first vision of the enrapturing beauty all round us, I think we will hunt up John and say, "John, why didn't you tell us it was so beautiful?" And John will say, "I tried to tell you when I wrote the twenty-first and twenty-second chapters of the last book in the Bible after I got my vision, but I couldn't do it."[108]

A poor woman once told the preacher Rowland Hill that the way to Heaven was short, easy and simple, comprising only three steps: out of self, into Christ and into Glory.

We need the Lord Jesus Christ as our personal Savior. There is no other way to Heaven.

Q 48. Which will have more people: Heaven or Hell?

A Because of something Jesus said in Matthew 7:13 and 14, I once thought that more people would be in Hell than in Heaven. He said, "Enter ye in at the strait gate: for wide is the gate, and broad is the way, that leadeth to destruction, and many there be which go in thereat: Because strait is the gate, and narrow is the way, which leadeth unto life, and few there be that find it." "Many" people go in the wide gate and travel on the broad way that leads to destruction, but "few" go in at the straight gate and travel on the narrow way that leads unto life. Then I realized statistics show that only about 2 percent of the people living today are saved and that about 90 percent of the church members in America are lost.

As I studied this question further, I learned some things that caused me to change my mind.

I learned that several anthropologists and sociologists have calculated that as many as 70 percent of all people never reach the age of eight. Disease, starvation, war, and so forth, kill them. The souls of most of these children go to live with the Lord. (See 2 Samuel 12:23; Matthew 18:1–6, 10; 19:14; Luke 18:15–17.) Furthermore, millions of babies are murdered by abortion—55 million worldwide and about 1.5 million in America each year. These victims of abortion will go to be with the Lord. Babies who die in the womb will also go to Heaven.

H. L. Willmington has estimated that approximately 40 billion people have lived on our planet.[109] Using that figure, let's look at some statistics:

28,000,000,000	(the 70 percent who died before reaching their eighth birthday)
990,000,000	(those killed by abortion since 1973—55,000,000 yearly multiplied by 18 years)
<u>240,000,000</u>	(those who are saved—2 percent of the 30 percent who reach the age of accountability)
29,230,000,000	Grand Total

If the figures are accurate, approximately 29 billion people (about three-fourths of all human beings) will enjoy the beauties of Heaven and the Holy City, New Jerusalem. I rejoice that so many will be there.

Preaching a sermon titled "Heaven and Hell" to 12,000 people, C. H. Spurgeon said:

> But my text [Matt. 8:11, 12] hath a yet greater depth of sweetness, for it says, that "many shall come and shall sit down." Some narrow-minded bigots think that heaven will be a very small place, where there will be a very few people, who went to their chapel or their church. I confess, I have no wish for a very small heaven, and I love to read in the Scriptures that there are many mansions in my Father's house. How often do I hear people say, "Ah! straight is the gate and narrow is the way, and few there be that find it. There will be very few in heaven; there will be most lost." My friend, I differ from you. Do you think that Christ will let the devil beat him? that he will let the devil have more in hell than there will be in heaven? No: it is impossible. For then Satan would laugh at Christ. There will be more in heaven than there are among the lost. God says that "there will be a number that no man can number who will be saved;" but he never says that there will be a number that no man can number that will be lost. There will be a host beyond all count who will get into heaven. What glad tidings for you and for me.[110]

Dr. Tim LaHaye encouraged us with these words: "Because the millennial population will undoubtedly exceed the total population during the whole time of biblical history, and since the majority living at that time will be Christians, it follows that there will be more people in heaven than in hell."[111]

Q 49. Can those who have died and gone to Heaven see us on the earth and know what we are doing?

A I know of no passage of Scripture that tells us that those who have gone to Heaven look down upon us on earth. If they could, I believe they would see many things that would trouble them greatly. They would see the sin and sorrow, tears and trouble, sufferings and heartaches of their loved ones and others on the earth. They would experience pain and hurt in their hearts because of what they saw.

Some people use Hebrews 12:1 and 2 to suggest that believers in Heaven watch us and that we run our race in an arena surrounded by those in Heaven who care about our running the race well. This passage does not say that those who have passed on are looking down from Heaven, but simply that we on earth are surrounded by a company of witnesses, the heroes of faith mentioned in chapter 11 of Hebrews.

Dr. Herbert Lockyer commented on this passage:

The word "witnesses" does not and cannot mean spectators. The Greek word for "witness" used here is martus *from which we have "martyr." These were men and women whose lives witnessed to the power of faith. Had the writer meant "spectators" he would have used* Autoptes *(Luke 1:2) or* Epoptes *(2 Pet. 1:16).*

Scripture, however, is silent on the question of Heaven being cognizant of earth, and our present welfare being the concern of dear ones above; it is best to follow the silence of Scripture and await the future.[112]

Q 50. If Christ is preparing Heaven for believers now, how can those who have died already be in Heaven?

A Jesus promised His disciples in John 14:2, "I go to prepare a place for you." He returned to Heaven to prepare a real place for His own. In Hebrews 11:16 we are told, "He hath prepared for them a city." The place He prepared is the holy city, New Jerusalem, "prepared as a bride adorned for her husband" (Rev. 21:2). This is the city for which Abraham looked, "a city which hath foundations, whose builder and maker is God" (Heb. 11:10), "the city of the living God, the heavenly Jerusalem" (Heb. 12:22) and the beautiful city described in Revelation 21:10–27, which will eventually come down from Heaven and dwell on the new earth (Rev. 21:2, 10).

Dr. Henry Morris wrote the following about this city:

> *Difficult though it may be, in the sophistication of our modern scientism, to believe such a thing, the Scriptures taken literally as they were meant to be taken, do teach that there is even now a great city being built by Christ far out in space somewhere. To this city go the spirits of all who die in Christ, there to await His return to earth. When He comes back, He will bring the holy city with Him and set it up for a time in earth's atmospheric heavens, perhaps orbiting the earth. There will be established His judgment seat, as well as the heavenly temple and its altar, to which John frequently refers in Revelation. The resurrected and raptured saints will dwell in this city, though with occasional visits to the earth, during the tribulation and millennial periods. Finally, when the earth is made new again, never to undergo any of the effects of God's curse or His judgments any more, the Lord Jesus Christ will bring it down to the earth where it will remain forever....*
>
> *The city had been "prepared" (Greek hetoimazo) completely by God Himself. This is the same word used by the Lord Jesus when He told His disciples, "I go to prepare a place for you" (John 14:2). It is also recorded in Hebrews 11:16: "He hath prepared for them a city."[113]*

Arthur W. Pink presented another thought concerning the preparation of a place:

> *We also understand this to mean that the Lord Jesus has procured the right—by His death on the Cross—for every believing sinner to enter Heaven. He has "prepared" for us a place there by entering Heaven as our Representative and taking possession of it on behalf of His people. As our Forerunner He marched in, leading captivity*

captive, and there planted His banner in the land of glory. He has
"prepared" for us a place there by entering the "holy of holies" on
High as our great High Priest, carrying our names in with Him.
Christ would do all that was necessary to secure for His people a
welcome and permanent place in Heaven.[114]

Q 51. When will God wipe away all tears?

A In answering this question, I checked the Bible to see what it says about tears. I was surprised to find that it has many references to tears and weeping. I counted more than 160 references to the words "weep," "weeping," "weepest," "weepeth" and "wept." I found 36 references to the word "tears."

Job said, "Mine eye poureth out *tears* unto God" (Job 16:20).

David wrote, "I water my couch with my *tears*" (Ps. 6:6). "My *tears* have been my meat day and night" (Ps. 42:3). "Put thou my *tears* into thy bottle" (Ps. 56:8). "They that sow in *tears* shall reap in joy" (Ps. 126:5).

Jeremiah lamented, "Oh that my head were waters, and mine eyes a fountain of *tears,* that I might weep day and night for the slain of the daughter of my people!" (Jer. 9:1). He also wrote, "That our eyes may run down with *tears*" (9:18), and "Mine eyes do fail with *tears*" (Lam. 2:11).

A woman began to wash Christ's feet with tears (Luke 7:38).

Paul served the Lord with many tears (Acts 20:19). He warned every one night and day with tears (Acts 20:31). He wrote to the Corinthians with many tears (2 Cor. 2:4). Paul was mindful of Timothy's tears (2 Tim. 1:4).

Jesus Christ offered up prayers and supplications with strong crying and tears (Heb. 5:7).

Though many people have wept much, and although many tears are being shed now, thank God for the promise that "God shall wipe away all tears from their eyes" (Rev. 7:17). "And God shall wipe away all tears from their eyes; and there shall be no more death, neither sorrow, nor crying, neither shall there be any more pain: for the former things are passed away" (Rev. 21:4). God will fulfill this promise when the first heaven and the first earth pass away and He creates the new heaven and new earth. This change will take place at the close of the Millennium and the beginning of the eternal state. At that time the holy city, New Jerusalem, will come down from God out of heaven, and God Himself will dwell with His people forever (Rev. 21:1–4). Not another tear will ever be shed. "He will swallow up death in victory; and the Lord GOD will wipe away tears from off all faces; and the rebuke of his people shall he take away from off all the earth: for the LORD hath spoken it" (Isa. 25:8).

Q 52. Without the Devil around for 1,000 years, will sin still exist?

A When Christ returns to earth, the Devil will be bound and cast into the bottomless pit for 1,000 years (Rev. 20:1–3). He will not be on the earth to tempt people to sin.

We believers have three main enemies: the world, the flesh and the Devil. The people who go into the Millennium will all be saved, but their children will be born with a sinful nature. Though the Devil will not be here to tempt anyone, and though Jesus Christ will rule righteously and will not tempt anyone, the flesh will still be around to tempt people to sin. Jesus Christ will judge those who sin in the Millennium: "And with the breath of his lips shall he slay the wicked" (Isa. 11:4). Zechariah tells us that during the Millennium those who will not come to Jerusalem to worship the King, the Lord of hosts, "even upon them shall be no rain. . . . This shall be the punishment of Egypt, and the punishment of all nations that come not up to keep the feast of tabernacles" (Zech. 14:17, 19).

Dr. Leon Wood wrote about sin in the Millennium:

Sin will not be nearly as prevalent as today, and it will not be accepted by society nor considered normal. Certainly it will not take the flagrant forms now found. But still it will be present, as several considerations show. First, living saints will not yet have their glorified bodies, which means that their bodies will be subject to passions and lusts. Second, the very fact that Satan will need to be bound indicates that people will still have natures to which he could appeal. Third, Christ is said to rule with a rod of iron (Ps. 2:9), reproving "with equity for the meek of the earth" (Isa. 11:4; cf. Ps.

72:1–4; Isa. 29:20, 21; 65:20; 66:24; Zech. 14:16–21); this shows that disobedience in some degree will occur. Fourth, that Satan will be able to find sympathizers to form an army at the very close of the age with which to make a final attack on the hosts of Christ (Rev. 20:7–9) indicates that some people will then live who will be openly rebellious against Christ.

This is evidence not only that sin will exist, but that some persons will not profess to be followers of Christ. In other words, there will be some unsaved in that day. Surely they will constitute a small minority, but still they will live and be apt subjects for Satan's final influence.[115]

Q 53. Do you think the things happening in the Middle East signal the end of time?

A The Middle East plays an extremely important part in prophecy. The Bible describes the Middle East as "in the midst of the land" or "the navel of the earth" (Ezek. 38:12). In Ezekiel 5:5 God claims, "This is Jerusalem: I have set it in the midst of the nations and countries that are round about her."

The Middle East has an interesting history and will have an interesting future.

The Middle East in God's Program

1. God created man in the Middle East (Gen. 2:7–15).
   God created Adam and placed him in the Garden of Eden, near the Euphrates River.
2. The fall of man occurred in the Middle East (Gen. 3:1–19).
   The first sin committed by man happened in the Middle East.
3. God gave the first promise of a Savior in the Middle East (Gen. 3:15).
4. The first child was born in the Middle East (Gen. 4:1).
5. The first murder was committed in the Middle East (Gen. 4:8).
6. The first city was built in the Middle East (Gen. 4:17).
7. God called Abraham, the father of the faithful, to the Middle East (Gen. 12:1–5).
8. Jesus Christ was born in the Middle East (Matt. 2:1).

9. Jesus Christ lived in the Middle East (Matt. 2:20–23).
10. Jesus Christ ministered in the Middle East (Luke 4:1, 14–21).
11. Jesus Christ died in the Middle East (Luke 23:26–33).
12. Jesus Christ rose from the dead in the Middle East (Matt. 28:1–8).
13. The Holy Spirit came to the Middle East (Acts 2:1–11).
14. The gospel was preached first in the Middle East (Acts 2:14–39).
15. Jesus Christ will come back to the Middle East (Acts 1:6–12; Zech. 14:4).
16. The three major battles yet to be fought will take place in the Middle East: the Battle of Gog and Magog (Ezek. 38; 39), the Battle of Armageddon (Rev. 16:16; 19:11–21) and the battle at the close of the Millennium (Rev. 20:7–9).
17. Jesus Christ will rule the world from the Middle East (Luke 1:30–33; Rev. 20:4–6).

The return of the Jews to their ancient land in the Middle East is one indication that Jesus will come soon. The revival of Israel and the formation of the state of Israel on May 14, 1948, are significant. Shortly after the Rapture, Israel will confirm a covenant with the Antichrist and rebuild her temple.

Dr. Walvoord commented, "If the rapture occurs before the signing of this covenant, as many premillennial scholars believe, it follows that the establishment of Israel in the land as a preparation for this covenant is a striking evidence that the rapture itself may be very near."[116]

In about the middle of the seven-year tribulation period, Russia will invade the Middle East (Ezek. 38; 39). Today, for the first time in world history, Russia could invade the Middle East and fulfill this prophecy. This fact also indicates that Christ's coming is near.

The Bible predicts that at the end of this age, four great world powers will surround Israel. The great power to the north is Russia. To the south of Israel will be another power, Egypt. This power is ready to play her part now. To the east of Israel will be a powerful nation, China. She is now in place and ready to march to Armageddon. Finally, there will be a world power, the Western ten nations of Europe. Each of these four powers now exists and awaits the proper time to act in fulfillment of Scripture.

These things, and others that I could name, are sure signs that Christ's coming is near, even "at the door."

Q 54. In what order will future events take place?

A Dr. M. R. DeHaan said many years ago, "Not one in a hundred of the members of our evangelical churches could give the order of events of the last days, and hence do not know what to look for."[117] Certainly new converts want to know what will happen next. A small group of newly converted Red Indians in northwest Canada went to a missionary and requested of him, "We are always hearing what God has done; now we want to know what He is going to do."

Some more mature Christians have little knowledge of God's time table for future events. Many believers are like the Christian businessman in North Carolina who said to me after I had preached on prophecy for a week in his church: "Before these meetings I was a panmillennialist."

"A what?" I asked.

"A panmillennialist."

I asked him, "Sir, what is a panmillennialist?"

He replied, "I figured that everything was going to pan out all right."

God is the author of the future, and He has told us some of the things that will take place. In Isaiah 46:9 and 10 we read, "I am God, and there is none like me. Declaring the end from the beginning, and from ancient times the things that are not yet done, saying, My counsel shall stand, and I will do all my pleasure."

God will send His Son to receive His own—the Rapture. This event is next on God's schedule. It could take place today (John 14:1–3; 1 Cor. 15:51, 52; 1 Thess. 4:13–18).

God the Son will judge His own—the Judgment Seat of Christ. Christians will meet the Lord in the air and immediately appear before the Judgment Seat of Christ (Rom. 14:10–12; 1 Cor. 3:9–15; 2 Cor. 5:10).

He will judge this world—the Tribulation Period. A seven-year tribulation period will take place on the earth, during which God will judge the unsaved people in twenty-one judgments. During this time, Russia will invade the Middle East; the Antichrist will appear; and the Battle of Armageddon will be fought (Dan. 9:24–27; Ezek. 38; 39; Matt. 24:21, 22; Rev. 6—19).

He will send His Son to rule this earth—the Millennium. At the close of the tribulation period, Jesus will come to earth and rule the earth for 1,000 years (Rev. 19:11–21; 20:1–7).

He will burn up the world—the New Heavens and New Earth. At the close of the Millennium, God will burn up this world and will create new heavens and a new earth (Isa. 65:17; 66:22; 2 Pet. 3:10–13; Rev. 21:1).

He will judge all of the unsaved at the final judgment—the Great White Throne Judgment. All of the wicked dead will be raised and will stand at the Great White Throne to be judged (John 5:22, 27; Acts 17:31; Rom. 2:16; Rev. 20:11–15).

He will dwell with His people forever—the Eternal State. In the eternal state God will dwell with His people in the beautiful holy city, New Jerusalem (Rev. 21:2–27; 22:1–5).

These things will surely come to pass because God promised, "I have spoken it, I will also bring it to pass; I have purposed it, I will also do it" (Isa. 46:11).

Q 55. Will the great earthquake referred to in Revelation 16:18 take place at the same time Christ touches the Mount of Olives, or will it take place earlier?

A Three times the New Testament records Jesus' prediction that "earthquakes shall be in divers places" (Matt. 24:7; Mark 13:8; Luke 21:11). God uses earthquakes to speak to and warn people. Many earthquakes have occurred in different places through the years. They have caused great damage and loss of life and will continue to do so.

Major earthquakes either took place or will take place at the following times and for the following reasons:

At the Giving of the Law. "And mount Sinai was altogether on a smoke, because the LORD descended upon it in fire: and the smoke thereof ascended as the smoke of a furnace, and the whole mount quaked greatly" (Exod. 19:18). This earthquake occurred when God descended upon Mount Sinai to give Moses the Law, the Ten Commandments. The earthquake was meant to teach man to have solemn respect for God's holy law.

At the Ending of the Law. The law ended with Jesus Christ's death on the cross.

Jesus, when he had cried again with a loud voice, yielded up the ghost. And, behold, the vail of the temple was rent in twain from the top to the bottom; and the earth did quake, and the rocks rent; and the graves were opened; and many bodies of the saints which slept arose, and came out of the graves after his resurrection, and went into the holy city, and appeared unto many. Now when the centurion, and they that were with him, watching Jesus, saw the earthquake, and those things that were done, they feared greatly, saying, Truly this was the Son of God (Matt. 27:50–54).

A mighty earthquake accompanied this closing event of the law so that man might fear God and not take His grace lightly.

At the Resurrection of Christ. "And, behold, there was a great earthquake: for the angel of the Lord descended from heaven, and came and rolled back the stone from the door, and sat upon it" (Matt. 28:2). The earthquake at this time was to show the people the mighty power of God.

At the Conversion of the Philippian Jailor. "And suddenly there was a great earthquake, so that the foundations of the prison were shaken: and immediately all the doors were opened, and every one's bands were loosed" (Acts 16:26).

When Russia Invades the Middle East. "And it shall come to pass at the same time when Gog shall come against the land of Israel, saith the Lord GOD, that my fury shall come up in my face. For in my jealousy and in the fire of my wrath have I spoken, Surely in that day there shall be a great shaking in the land of Israel" (Ezek. 38:18, 19). God will be angry and send an earthquake. Men shall shake at His presence (v. 20).

At the Opening of the Sixth Seal. "And I beheld when he had opened the sixth seal, and, lo, there was a great earthquake; and the sun became black as sackcloth of hair, and the moon became as blood" (Rev. 6:12). Someone has said this will be the world's greatest prayer meeting—when men pray to the mountains and rocks to fall on them rather than face the Lord Jesus Christ (vv. 15–17).

At the Beginning of the Seven Trumpet Judgments. "And the angel took the censer, and filled it with fire of the altar, and cast it into the earth: and there were voices, and thunderings, and lightnings, and an earthquake" (Rev. 8:5).

At the Second Woe. "And the same hour was there a great earthquake, and the tenth part of the city fell, and in the earthquake were slain of men seven thousand: and the remnant were affrighted, and gave glory to the God of heaven" (Rev. 11:13).

At the Blowing of the Seventh Trumpet. "And the temple of God was opened in heaven, and there was seen in his temple the ark of his testament: and there were lightnings, and voices, and thunderings, and an earthquake, and great hail" (Rev. 11:19).

At the Pouring Out of the Seventh Vial. "And there were voices, and thunders, and lightnings; and there was a great earthquake, such as was not since men were upon the earth, so mighty an earthquake, and so great" (Rev. 16:18).

This earthquake is said to be the greatest of all earthquakes. The great city Jerusalem will be divided into three parts, the cities of the nations will fall, Babylon will be judged, every island will disappear, the mountains will not be found and hailstones weighing a talent (about 100 pounds) will fall upon people (vv. 19–21).

Dr. Henry Morris wrote concerning the hailstones:

> *These rocks are not mere pebbles, but boulders. Each one on the average weighs a "talent," which is an ancient, and somewhat variable, unit of weight, always on the order of 100 pounds or more. We are to visualize, therefore, a rain of 100-pound boulders pelting down from the sky, along with the greatest earthquake of all time.*[118]

At the Second Coming of Christ. "And his feet shall stand in that day upon the mount of Olives, which is before Jerusalem on the east, and the mount of Olives shall cleave in the midst thereof toward the east and toward the west, and there shall be a very great valley; and half of the mountain shall remove toward the north, and half of it toward the south" (Zech. 14:4). When Christ comes to earth at the close of the Tribulation, His feet will stand on the Mount of Olives. The Mount of Olives will split in two because of the great earthquake at that time.

The order of events is as follows: first, the great earthquake will occur at the pouring out of the seventh vial; shortly afterward, Christ will come to earth and touch His feet on the Mount of Olives.

The Bible predicts, "And they shall go into the holes of the rocks, and into the caves of the earth, for fear of the LORD, and for the glory of his majesty, when he ariseth to shake terribly the earth" (Isa. 2:19).

Warren Wiersbe has written these challenging and encouraging words: "God today is shaking things. (Have you read the newspapers lately?) He wants to tear down the 'scaffolding' and reveal the unshakable realities that are eternal. Alas, too many people (including Christians) are building their lives on things that can shake."[119]

Q 56. How will Egypt relate with Israel in the future?

A Isaiah 19:16–25 gives an outstanding prophecy concerning Egypt, Assyria and Israel in a future time called "that day" (vv. 16, 18, 19, 21, 23, 24). "That day" is the day or period of time that will accompany the events surrounding the second coming of Christ and the following Millennium. From the birth of the nation of Israel until today, no other nation has persecuted the Jews so long and so violently as Egypt has. Yet in this passage God promised to bless Egypt and called her "my people" (v. 25).

Here are some of the things that will happen in "that day":

1. Egypt will be afraid because of Judah and the shaking of the hand of the Lord (vv. 16, 17).
2. Egypt will be converted (v. 18). The land of Egypt will speak the language of Canaan and swear to the Lord, meaning they will embrace the faith of Israel and bind themselves to the Lord to honor Him by solemn covenant and oath.
3. True worship will be instituted (vv. 19–22). They will erect an altar and a pillar to the Lord as a sign and a witness that they are worshiping the God of Israel. Egypt will cry unto the Lord, and He will send them a Savior to deliver them. They will know the Lord. God will first smite Egypt and then heal her. Dr. John F. Walvoord wrote, "This situation was almost unbelievable for the people of Judah in Isaiah's day. But it will occur. It will take place after the Messiah has returned and established His millennial kingdom."[120]
4. God will make Israel, Egypt and Assyria (modern Iraq) a blessing in the midst of the earth (vv. 23–25). Egypt will be called "my people," Iraq will be called "the work of my hands," and Israel will be called "mine inheritance."

Dr. Walter Kaiser said:

The whole thing staggers the mind . . . God's triumph will not only include all nations, but some of the most hostile and bitter of enemies. Jews, Arabs and Egyptians will go to the house of God together to worship again!... The future for Israel, Egypt and Iraq (to name just those dealt with here) is bright indeed. God will have success.[121]

Q 57. Does Israel now occupy the land promised to them?

A God told Abraham, "Get thee out of thy country, and from thy kindred, and from thy father's house, unto a land that I will shew thee," and the Bible tells us that he left his land with his wife and Lot, "and into the land of Canaan they came" (Gen. 12:1, 5). To the descendants of Abraham God gave the entire land from the river of Egypt (not the Nile River, but Wadi el-Arish) to the Euphrates River (Gen. 15:18), and they are the rightful owners of the entire land of Canaan. This land covers a large area and includes most of the Sinai Peninsula, Edom, Transjordan, Negev, Syria and, in general, the areas occupied by the Arabian nations.

The Bible refers to Palestine (modern Israel) as "the Lord's land" (Hos. 9:3) and "the land of promise" (Heb. 11:9). God Himself called it "my land" (2 Chron. 7:20; Jer. 2:7; 16:18). Scores of Old Testament passages refer to this land as being given by God to Israel, and they often state that Israel will have it forever (Gen. 13:15; 17:8; Deut. 4:40; Isa. 60:21; Jer. 7:7; 25:5).

God predicted that the Jews would disobey Him, be driven out of Canaan and scattered among the nations. "And I will bring the land [Canaan] into desolation: and your enemies which dwell therein shall be astonished at it. And I will scatter you among the heathen, and will draw out a sword after you: and your land shall be desolate, and your cities waste" (Lev. 26:32, 33).

This prophecy was literally fulfilled in 721 B.C., when the northern ten tribes were carried into captivity by Assyria, and in 586 B.C., when the two southern tribes were taken into Babylon. About 50,000 Israelites returned seventy years later, but the rest were scattered throughout the whole earth. In A.D. 70, Jerusalem was utterly destroyed and the remnant was dispersed among the nations. God promised them:

For I will take you from among the heathen, and gather you out of all countries, and will bring you into your own land. . . . A new heart also will I give you. . . . And I will put my spirit within you. . . . And ye shall dwell in the land that I gave to your fathers; and ye shall be my people, and I will be your God. . . . This land that was desolate is become like the garden of Eden. . . . I the LORD have spoken it, and I will do it. . . . And they shall know that I am the LORD (Ezek. 36:24, 26–28, 35, 36, 38).

Israel has never yet possessed all of the land God gave them, but the passage above promises that God will gather them, bring them into the land, give them a new heart and put His Spirit in them. It also promises that they will dwell in the land God gave them (all of it). The land will become like the Garden of Eden. They will be God's people, and God will be their God. "I the LORD have spoken it, and I will do it."

Q 58. Will we eat food at the Marriage Supper of the Lamb?

A When Jesus comes for His own at the Rapture, every Christian will go to be with Him (1 Cor. 15:51, 52; 1 Thess. 4:16, 17). We will meet Him in the air. The Judgment Seat of Christ will take place first (2 Cor. 5:10). After the Judgment Seat of Christ, the Church will be married to Christ (Rev. 19:7). Following the marriage, the marriage supper of the Lamb will take place (Rev. 19:9). Some people believe the marriage supper will take place in Heaven; others believe it will be held on earth. "The marriage takes place in Heaven, but it would seem that the marriage supper occurs on the earth, the latter when the Bridegroom returns with His Bride."[122]

Pentecost wrote, ". . . It may be best to take the latter view and view the marriage of the Lamb as that event in the heavens in which the church is eternally united to Christ and the marriage feast or supper as the millennium, to which Jews and Gentiles will be invited, which takes place on the earth. . . ."[123]

Harold Willmington wrote:

In New Testament times the length and cost of this supper was determined by the wealth of the father. Therefore, when his beloved Son is married, the Father of all grace (whose wealth is unlimited) will rise to the occasion by giving his Son and the bride a hallelujah celebration which will last for a thousand years![124]

The Bride is made up of the Jews and Gentiles who have been saved during the Age of Grace (Acts 15:14; 1 Cor. 12:13); the invited guests are the Old Testament saints who will be resurrected at the end of the Tribulation (John 3:28, 29; Dan. 12:1, 2) plus the vast throng of Jews and Gentiles who will be saved during the tribulation period (Rev. 7).

René Pache wrote concerning the feast, "Every marriage has its feast. The guests rejoice with the happy pair, and they all have fellowship together around a sumptuously laden table."[125]

The church saints, along with the invited guests, will also "have fellowship together around a sumptuously laden table." Concerning the supper, J. A. Seiss wrote:

Of what that supper shall consist we cannot yet know. The Scriptures speak of bread of heaven and angel's food, and the Saviour tells of eating and drinking there. He who supplied the wedding at Cana, and fed the thousands in the wilderness, and furnished the little dinner to His worn disciples as they came up from the sea of toil to the shore trodden by His glorified feet, can be at no loss to make good every word, and letter, and allusion which the Scriptures contain with reference to that high festival. The angels know something about it, and the angel told John that it will be a blessed thing to be there. "Write," said the heavenly voice, "write, Blessed are they who have been called to the supper of the marriage of the Lamb [Rev. 19:9]."[126]

At one time after His resurrection, Jesus appeared to His disciples. They were terrified because they supposed they had seen a spirit. He asked them for something to eat, and they gave Him a piece of broiled fish and a honeycomb. He ate it in their presence (Luke 24:36–43). The Bible promises us believers that our resurrected bodies will be like His: "For our conversation [citizenship] is in heaven; from whence also we look for the Saviour, the Lord Jesus Christ: Who shall change our vile body, that it may be fashioned like unto his glorious body . . ." (Phil. 3:20, 21). As Jesus ate in His resurrected body, so will His saints. I am sure we will also have His

Word throughout eternity as our food—food for thought—and we will be filled with His Word. But we shall also eat food at the marriage supper of the Lamb.

> [The Bible mentions four suppers.] God invites you to the first three, but not to the fourth. If you accept His invitation to the first, you may go to the second, and you will be at the third but not at the fourth.
>
> Do you know what the first supper is? "A certain man made a great supper"; but only "the maimed, and the halt, and the blind" were persuaded to attend (Luke 14:16–24). That supper was used to typify the supper of salvation. It comes in this age. And why is it called "supper" instead of "dinner" or "breakfast" or "lunch"? Because supper is the last meal of the day, even as "the great supper of God" will be the last meal of that coming day. We eat our supper; the sun goes down; night falls; the shadows lengthen. So also, when this Age of Grace—this supper of salvation—is over, the night will descend upon the world.
>
> The second supper is the Lord's Supper, where the believer partakes of the emblems that represent the broken body and the shed blood of the Son of God. If you have accepted the invitation to the first supper, you have a right to sit at the table when the second is served. And if you are a Christian, you will surely be at the third, which we have already described, "the marriage supper of the Lamb."
>
> And what is the fourth? Ah, it is that dreadful feast to which the angel "standing in the sun" invited the "fowls that fly in the midst of heaven" [Rev. 19:17].
>
> My friend, you do not want to be at that dreadful supper. But you will be unless you "believe on the Lord Jesus Christ." God Almighty says that every unregenerated man who eats of the sacred emblems at the Lord's Table and drinks the wine, drinks and eats condemnation to himself. If you reject the invitation to the first, the supper of salvation, going to the second will avail you nothing; you will not be present at the third, the marriage supper of the Lamb; but you will surely be at the fourth, that last and dreadful "supper of God."[127]

Q 59. Do all of the seven types of churches in Revelation 2 and 3 exist today?

A The letters to the seven churches of Revelation 2 and 3 are letters to churches that existed in Asia Minor in the first century. First, they were written to rebuke, encourage, warn, instruct and help the churches in existence. Second, they were written to give us a picture of seven different kinds of churches during the entire Church Age and to carry a spiritual message for churches at any time. Third, these letters present to us church history in seven different stages, from the close of the Apostolic Age to the end of the Dispensation of Grace. Each of the seven letters represents a different phase of that history.

- Ephesus stood for the Church of the first century.
- Smyrna represented the persecuted Church of the second and third centuries.
- Pergamos was the Church from about A.D. 312 to A.D. 500.
- Thyatira represents the Church of the Dark Ages from the sixth century on through the fifteenth.
- Sardis describes for us the rise and development and finally the corruption of Protestantism.
- Philadelphia pictures for us the Church of the revival of the nineteenth century.
- Laodicea is the end-time Church of apostasy.

Some churches today are like the church at Ephesus and have left their first love. Other churches today face persecution, like the church at Smyrna. Some churches are worldly, like the church at Pergamos. Some are tolerant, like the church at Thyatira. And some, like the church at Sardis, are dead today. Some of today's churches are true, like the church at Philadelphia, and some are lukewarm, like the church at Laodicea.

Q 60. Why do people say the Babylon spoken of in the latter days means the United States? What role will the U.S. play in prophecy?

A Students of the Word of God have for a long time diligently tried to ascertain the answer to this question. Some think that the United States may be the nation referred to as "political Babylon" in Revelation 18. Others think that Biblical prophecy never names the United States, although the U.S. would obviously play a role in prophecy just as any other nation in the world would. Dr. S. Franklin Logsdon, who has written several items on the subject, takes the former position. The gist of his teaching is this:

- There was an historical Babylon (Gen. 11).
- There is an ecclesiastical Babylon (Rev. 17).
- There is a political Babylon (Rev. 18).

Historical Babylon is symbolized by a monumental tower, ecclesiastical Babylon by a mystical woman and political Babylon by a mighty city. In the case of historical Babylon, God felled the tower, confounded the tongues and scattered the people. In the case of ecclesiastical or religious Babylon, the Antichrist will hate the harlot, outlaw religion and finally destroy the false church. In the case of political Babylon, trials will plague the earth, the economy will crash and the great city will be made desolate.

I am now quoting from Dr. Logsdon's book, *Is the U.S.A. in Prophecy?*

> *Quoting from Jeremiah 50:45, we read, "Therefore hear ye the counsel of the Lord that he hath taken against Babylon." Of course He does not here suggest we argue the matter, or advance our opinions, or evolve a spectacular thesis. No, He merely requests us to hear His counsel that He has taken against a certain Babylon, which, to all intents and purposes, appears to be an endtime nation, spiritually called Babylon. This counsel is prolifically stated in Jeremiah 50 and 51 and in Revelation 18.*

> *. . . There is a striking resemblance between the recorded characteristics of prophetical Babylon and the U.S.A. This will be generally agreed. Some characteristics, however, are more convincing than others. Some are more tenable than others. In the end, they may only strike the reader as an analogy; but, taken as a whole, the consideration is very thought-provoking, and, conceivably, when all the mysteries are unfolded, could prove the U.S.A. to be the very national entity God has in mind.*[128]

Dr. Charles L. Feinberg took the opposite position. Feinberg maintained that Biblical prophecy does not mention the United States:

First, we must cleave strictly to Scripture statements, not inferences and beggings of the question. The place to begin in Bible geography is not even the Garden of Eden. It is with Deuteronomy 32:8: "When the Most High gave the nations their inheritance, when He separated the sons of man, He set the boundaries of the peoples according to the number of the sons of Israel" (NASB).

The focal point of all God's dealings with man on earth is the land of promise. There God made His greatest investment for man's salvation through the sacrifice of His Son. There He expects to climax and consummate all His purposes in time (see Ps. 2:6). There is no more strategically located area on the face of the globe. Ezekiel referred to it as "the center of the world" (38:12: Heb., "navel"). It sits at the confluence of three continents and between the most densely populated land masses on earth, Europe and Southeast Asia.

Second, in the panoramic view of world empires in the Book of Daniel there is no hint of any nation in this hemisphere (see Dan. 2, 7, 9).

Third, it is always dangerous to judge future events principally on the events of a single period in history. The dominant power in the world in the last century was England; it is so no longer. America is prominent now, but there is no assurance how long her diminishing influence will last.

Fourth, we need not expect every great national power in history to be included in the prophetic Scriptures. Where are India and China prominent in prophecy, two of the most populous nations on earth?

Fifth, more than a modicum of Scriptures in every one of the major prophets and a number of the minor prophets speak in unison of the time when all *the nations will be embroiled in a universal confederacy against God and His people. How, in this day of interdependence of all nations, could the United States fail to be involved? Was she not in World War I, World War II, Korea, Vietnam, Cambodia and others? Even if she determined on an isolationist policy in world affairs, could she possibly carry it through?*

To ask the question is to answer it. Yes, America will be involved in prophetic events, but nowhere by name. Why not? The answer is in Deuteronomy 29:29.

When a young preacher came to C. H. Spurgeon with a bag of imponderable questions for a clear answer from the prince of preachers, the latter wisely answered: "Young man, you are going to have to let God know some things you do not know."[129]

Whatever the role of the United States in Bible prophecy (or lack thereof), we should remember God's hatred for sin. Dr. John F. Walvoord gave this sober warning: "History has many records of great nations that have risen to unusual power and influence only to decline because of internal corruption or international complications. It may well be that the United States of America is today at the zenith of its power much as Babylon was in the sixth century B.C. prior to its sudden downfall at the hands of Medes and Persians (Daniel 5)."[130]

Q 61. Why will the nations need the healing leaves of the tree of life in the New Jerusalem (Rev. 22:2)?

A Dr. Lehman Strauss said of Revelation 22:2, "This is a difficult passage, and I prefer to leave it for the present."[131]

I will try to answer this question, although I agree with Dr. Strauss that the passage is difficult. The tree of life spoken of in this passage seems to allude to a similar tree in the Garden of Eden (Gen. 3:22, 24). God kept it from man after he sinned, but God will give it back to His children. It will bear twelve different kinds of fruits, one for each month of the year, and its leaves are for "the healing of the nations." People ask, "Why should healing be necessary in eternity?" Dr. John F. Walvoord gave an enlightening answer:

The word for "healing" is therapeian, from which the English word therapeutic *is derived, almost directly transliterated from the Greek. Rather than specifically meaning "healing," it should be understood as "health-giving," as the word in its root meaning has the idea of serving or ministering. In other words, the leaves of the tree promote the enjoyment of life in the new Jerusalem, and are not for correcting ills which do not exist. This, of course, is confirmed by the fact that there is no more curse as indicated in verse 3. . . .*

The intimation of this passage is that while it is not necessary for believers in the eternal state to sustain life in any way by physical means, they can enjoy that which the tree provides.[132]

Q 62. Are "the times of the Gentiles" and "the fulness of the Gentiles" the same?

A Jesus spoke of the Times of the Gentiles in Luke 21:24: "And they shall fall by the edge of the sword, and shall be led away captive into all nations: and Jerusalem shall be trodden down of the Gentiles, until the times of the Gentiles be fulfilled." The Times of the Gentiles began when Nebuchadnezzar, king of Babylon, sent his armies against Judah, about 600 B.C., destroyed Jerusalem and took many Jews into captivity. Since then, Jerusalem has been under the dominion of Gentile authority and will continue to be under Gentile authority until the end of the tribulation period. At that time the Lord Jesus Christ will come in glory, bring to an end the Times of the Gentiles and set up His kingdom and rule on this earth for 1,000 years.

Paul spoke of the fullness of the Gentiles in Romans 11:25: "For I would not, brethren, that ye should be . . . wise in your own conceits; that blindness in part is happened to Israel, until the fulness of the Gentiles be come in." The "fulness of the Gentiles" refers to the people God is calling out from among the nations (the Gentiles) during this present Dispensation of Grace. These called-out ones (Acts 15:14) form the Church. When the last member is added to the Church, the Church will be complete and the "fulness of the Gentiles" will have come.

Paul VanGorder made the following distinction:

These two phases therefore describe two completely different subjects. The "times of the Gentiles" speaks of the political domination of the world by four great world powers; the "fullness

of the Gentiles" depicts that day when the church, the body of
Christ, is complete, and the focus of redemptive history shifts once
again to Israel.[133]

Dr. John Walvoord concurred with VanGorder. He wrote, "The times of the Gentiles began long before Christ and will continue until Christ returns to establish His kingdom. The fullness of the Gentiles began at Pentecost and will continue only as long as the present age of grace."[134]

Q 63. What does Revelation 22:19 mean? It says, "And if any man shall take away from the words of the book of this prophecy, God shall take away his part out of the book of life."

A The book of Revelation begins with a blessing pronounced on the one who reads, hears and keeps those things written in it (Rev. 1:3), and it closes with a curse upon those who tamper with it (Rev. 22:18, 19). Close to the beginning of the Bible (Deut. 4:2), near the middle (Prov. 30:6) and here at the end, God warns about adding to or taking away from the Bible. The threat does not mean that a child of God could be guilty of adding to or taking away from the Word of God. A true Christian would not do that. This solemn warning applies to critics who have tampered with and ridiculed the book of Revelation and other parts of the Bible as well. Those unbelievers will have no part in the Book of Life or the holy city or the things that are written in this book.

Oliver B. Greene wrote concerning those kinds of people:

Any person who tampers with Revelation (which a Spirit-filled, born again believer would not do) has cancelled his right to any part of eternal life and the joys of Heaven beyond the grave. He will burn in hell for tampering with the prophecies of the book of Revelation—or any other portion of God's holy Word.[135]

In a helpful article in *Grace Theological Journal,* Charles R. Smith wrote:

[Revelation] 22:19 is probably the most frequently cited verse in

support of the view that names may be blotted from the book of life. The support wholly vanishes, however, when one examines any recognized English version other than the KJV. It is well-known among Bible scholars that there is absolutely no Greek manuscript support for the KJV'S rendering of this verse. All of the Greek manuscripts have 'tree of life,' not 'book of life.' Rev. 22:18,19 simply affirms that unbelievers who rob this book of its authority by adding to it or by taking from it shall have the plagues of the book 'added to' them and the blessings of the book 'taken away' from them. Among the blessings to be withheld are access to the tree of life and to the holy city. The tree of life symbolizes the availability of eternal life in both the opening and closing paragraphs of the Bible. Therefore, though Rev. 22:19 may be difficult to understand, it cannot be used as a basis for any doctrine suggesting that names may be blotted from the book of life.[136]

Q 64. Can names be blotted out of the Book of Life?

A Revelation 3:5 records this promise: "He that overcometh, the same shall be clothed in white raiment; and I will not blot out his name out of the book of life, but I will confess his name before my Father, and before his angels." One portion of the verse bothers some people; it is "I will *not* blot out his name out of the book of life." Some infer from this statement that names can be blotted out of the Book of Life. The verse does not say that names will be blotted out of the Book of Life. In fact, it says just the opposite: "I will not blot out his name out of the book of life."

Of course, the statement implies the possibility of having one's name blotted out. J. A. Seiss in his book *Letters to the Seven Churches* stated, "There is a Celestial roll-book of all those who name the name of Jesus. But it depends on the persevering fidelity of the individual whether his name is to continue on that roll or to be blotted out."[137]

Dr. John F. Walvoord answered Seiss's conclusion by writing, "To make the continuance of our salvation depend upon works, however, is gross failure to comprehend that salvation is by grace alone. If it depended upon the believer's perseverance, the name would not have been written there in the first place."[138]

Quite a few Christians believe that everyone's name is written in the Book of Life at birth. Regarding this belief, Dr. Walvoord wrote:

> *As they come to maturity and are faced with the responsibility of accepting or rejecting Christ, their names are blotted out if they fail to receive Jesus Christ as Saviour; whereas those who do accept Christ as Saviour are confirmed in their position in the book of life, and their names are confessed before the Father and the heavenly angels.*[139]

Dr. Warren Wiersbe believes the following:

> *As unbelievers die, their names are removed from the book; thus, at the final judgment, the book contains only the names of believers (Rev. 20:12–15). It then becomes "the Lamb's Book of Life" (Rev. 21:27), because only those saved by the Lord Jesus Christ have their names in it. All the others have been blotted out, something God would never do for any true child of God.*[140]

God's Word makes it clear that all names are not written in the Book of Life. John speaks of those ". . . whose names were not written in the book of life from the foundation of the world" (Rev. 17:8).

Three verses in the Old Testament speak of blotting someone out of a book: Exodus 32:32 and 33 and Psalm 69:28. The psalmist calls the book "thy book which thou hast written" (v. 32). Psalm 69:28 calls it "the book of the living." Exodus 32:33 records God's words: "Whosoever hath sinned against me, him will I blot out of my book." None of the verses mentions the Book of Life. Charles R. Smith commented, "A much better approach is to understand these OT passages as metaphorical references to a book of covenant blessings."[141] Then he quoted J. B. Lightfoot: " . . . Hence to be blotted out of the book of the living means to forfeit the privileges of the theocracy; to be shut out from God's favor."[142]

The New Testament refers to the Book of Life eight times: Philippians 4:3; Revelation 3:5; 13:8; 17:8; 20:12,15; 21:27; and 22:19. In this Book of Life God has recorded the names of His elect. "According as he hath chosen us in him before the foundation of the world" (Eph. 1:4). In his book *Expanded Translation,* Dr. Kenneth Wuest wrote, "Your names have been written in heaven and are on permanent record up there."[143] Now if the names of God's children were written in Heaven before the foundation of the world (Rev. 17:8), and if God knows everything that will happen, would He write someone's name in His book only to turn around and one day blot it out? Jesus encourages His own with these wonderful words: ". . . Rejoice, because your names are written in heaven" (Luke 10:20).

I quote again from *The Book of Life* by Charles R. Smith:

> *This study has argued that the OT allusions to a register of names refer to those who are slated for covenant blessings, with a primary focus on the temporal blessings associated with physical life. These references do not convey the full import of the later NT statements regarding the Book of Life. However, they foreshadow the later significance. While names could be removed from a list of recipients of temporal, conditional covenantal blessings, names could never be removed from a list of recipients of eternal, unconditional covenantal blessings.*
>
> *On the basis of these considerations it may be concluded that there is only one Book of Life which lists the names of those who are chosen and predestined for eternal life. This book has never contained the names of all humans, or of all professing believers, or of "believers" who later "lose" their salvation, but only the names of all the elect. The names are not entered at birth or at the time of salvation, but were all entered "before the foundation of the world." These names are never blotted from this register.[144]*

Thank God that instead of our *names* being blotted out, He has promised, "Repent ye therefore, and be converted, that your *sins* may be blotted out . . ." (Acts 3:19).

Dr. S. Maxwell Coder clearly explained how we can know that our names are written in the Book of Life:

> *We can be sure our names are in the book of life as Paul was about the inclusion of Euodias and Syntche, of whom he wrote, "[their] names are in the book of life" (Phil. 4:3). Our names will never be blotted out if we have trusted Christ, sealing our faith by acknowledging Him in the presence of others.[145]*

Q 65. How are Gog and Magog present at the end of the thousand years?

A When I was in Trinidad for six weeks' ministry, a missionary heard I was speaking on prophecy, and he traveled a distance to ask me about this subject. Gog and Magog in Revelation 20:8 are not the same people as described in Ezekiel 38 and 39. The invading armies described in Ezekiel 38 and 39 will come from the north (38:15). In Revelation 20 they will assemble from the four corners of the earth (v. 8). In Ezekiel, Gog is the head of the armies; in Revelation, Satan gathers them (20:7, 8). In Ezekiel, the armies come to take a spoil, a prey, silver and gold, cattle and goods (38:13). In Revelation, they come to make war against the camp of the saints and the beloved city, Jerusalem (20:9). The battle in Ezekiel takes place before Armageddon; in the book of Revelation, it occurs after the Millennium. In Ezekiel, the invasion has at least eighteen results (38:13—39:13). Revelation records only one result: "Fire came down from God out of heaven, and devoured them" (20:9). In Ezekiel, the destruction is followed by a seven-month burial of the dead bodies (39:12). In Revelation, it is followed by the last judgment (20:11–15). Ezekiel does not mention Satan, but in Revelation, he is prominent (20:7–10).

Concerning the two passages, J. Dwight Pentecost wrote,

It has been demonstrated before that this rebellion cannot be identified with that invasion of Gog and Magog, described in Ezekiel 38 and 39, but bears the same name in that the purpose is identical in these two satanically motivated movements: to destroy the seat of theocratic power and the subjects of the theocracy.[146]

The Millennium will begin with only the righteous entering it. It will be earth's golden age, a time of peace and prosperity. As time goes by, children will be born. They will have sinful natures and will need to be saved just as people today. Many of them will be saved, but some of them will rebel against the righteous rule of Christ. Open rebellion will mean instant punishment. Consequently, many will render only feigned obedience to Him. Psalm 66:3 declares, "Say unto God, How terrible art thou in thy works! through the greatness of thy power shall thine enemies submit [yield feigned obedience] unto me."

They will abide by the rules of the kingdom of Christ only because they have to. Therefore, when the Devil is loosed from his prison at the close of the thousand years, he will gather a large number of them to join him in his last revolt against Christ.

Q 66. What did Peter mean when he wrote, "Take heed, as unto a light that shineth in a dark place, until the day dawn, and the day star arise in your hearts" (2 Pet. 1:19)?

A To "take heed" means "to give earnest attention to, to hold on to" the prophecies—to study them diligently, to meditate upon them and to obey them. We should "take heed" to the Bible because it is the Word of God, not of men. "For the prophecy came not in old time by the will of man: but holy men of God spake as they were moved by the Holy Ghost" (2 Pet. 1:21). We should take heed to the Scriptures because "We have also a more sure word of prophecy" (2 Pet. 1:19). Much of what has been prophesied has already been fulfilled, and the remainder is certain to be fulfilled.

Another reason we should take heed to the Scriptures is that they are like a "light that shineth in a dark place" (v. 19). The only true light man has in this world is the light of Scripture. Peter referred particularly to the Old Testament Scriptures, but this statement is true of the New Testament as well. This light is shining "in a dark place" (v. 19). "Dark" here means squalid and gloomy. Surely the world today is dark, squalid and gloomy. Look at the newspapers, the magazines, the TV programs, the social conditions, the moral conditions, the increasing lawlessness and selfishness, the divorce rate, the immorality, the drinking, the gambling, the use of illegal drugs and the desire for more sinful pleasure. Look at the nations preparing for war. Surely the world is a dark place. Paul wrote, "The night is far spent" (Rom. 13:12).

We are to take heed unto the Scriptures "until the day dawn, and the day star arise in [our] hearts" (2 Pet. 1:19), until that glorious day when the Lord Jesus Christ will come again. Revelation 22:16 calls Him the Morning Star, and Malachi 4:2 refers to Him as the Sun of Righteousness.

After Paul said, "The night is far spent," he added, "The day is at hand" (Rom. 13:12).

Dr. D. M. Lloyd-Jones wrote concerning the shining of the light,

"Not only that, the light is still there, the lamp is still shining. And what does it show? Here is the final statement. This process is to go on until Christ, the Messiah, the Son of God, shall again return to this world. He will come as a King. He will come as a Conqueror."[147]

Q 67. How will the 144,000 Israelites know their tribal lineage since the records were destroyed in A.D. 70, when Titus destroyed Jerusalem?

A The Bible makes it plain that twelve tribes of Israel still exist, because their names are given. Though Israelites today do not normally know what tribe they belong to, God knows.

Some men teach that the tribes of Israel are lost or that they are now the English-speaking people of the world.

Dr. Walvoord wrote of Israel, "Obviously none of the tribes are lost as far as God is concerned. Though genealogies have been lost, a modern Jew can be assured that he belongs to the seed of Abraham; and God knows into which tribe he should be classified."[148]

Q 68. Does God hear the prayers of the unsaved Jews?

A Nowhere in the Bible does God promise to hear and answer an unsaved person's prayer, either Jew or Gentile. We are to pray to God in the name of Jesus (John 16:23, 24). We can go to God only through Jesus Christ (John 14:6). John 9:31 says, "Now we know that God heareth not sinners: but if any man be a worshipper of God, and doeth his will, him he heareth."

In Acts 10 we find an unsaved Italian, Cornelius. He was a centurion, a devout man, a God-fearing man, a generous man and a praying man who wanted to be saved but didn't know how. As he prayed to God, the Lord heard his prayer and sent an angel to him. The angel said, "Thy prayers and thine alms are come up for a memorial before God" (v. 4). The angel instructed him to send for Peter, "Who shall tell thee words, whereby thou and all thy house shall be saved" (Acts 11:14). Peter went to the house of Cornelius and preached the

114

gospel to those assembled there. All of them were saved.

When a person wants to be saved, God will get the gospel to him. God has promised that "whosoever shall call upon the name of the Lord shall be saved" (Rom. 10:13). The repentant thief on the cross prayed, "Lord, remember me when thou comest into thy kingdom." Christ answered, "To day shalt thou be with me in paradise" (Luke 23:42, 43).

God will hear the prayer of the unsaved Jew or Gentile if that person trusts the Lord Jesus Christ as his personal Savior.

Q 69. Where does the Bible say that if we do not witness to people who are lost, their blood will be on our hands? What does that statement mean?

A This statement is found in Ezekiel 33:1–9, which teaches that we are responsible to witness to the lost. If we warn them of the danger of being lost and plead with them to turn from sin, and if they listen and trust Christ as their Savior, they will be saved and their souls will be delivered. If they do not listen when we warn them, they will die in their sin; but we have "delivered our souls," and their blood will be upon their own heads. But if we fail to warn them, they will die in their sin, and their blood will be upon our hands.

God has made us accountable for other people's lives, and we cannot escape that responsibility. If we see a man drowning and hear him calling for help, we are accountable to try to rescue him. We are responsible to help others, and we are responsible to try to get people saved by witnessing to them. God warns us in Proverbs 24:11 and 12: "If thou forbear to deliver them that are drawn unto death, and those that are ready to be slain; If thou sayest, Behold, we knew it not; doth not he that pondereth the heart consider it? and he that keepeth thy soul, doth not he know it? and shall not he render to every man according to his works?" Ninety-five percent of Christians in America never win a soul to Christ, and many of them never even try. At the Judgment Seat of Christ they will have to account for their failure to witness.

When Paul witnessed to the Jews in Corinth, most of them refused to believe the gospel, and Paul said to them, "Your blood be upon your own heads; I am clean" (Acts 18:6). Acts 20:25 and 26 record these words of Paul: "Wherefore I take you to record this day, that I am pure from the blood of all men. For I have not shunned to declare unto you all the counsel of God." He was free from guilt because he had delivered God's message.

David prayed, "Deliver me from blood guiltiness, O God" (Ps. 51:14). May God help us to pray that prayer. Then as God gives us opportunities, let us be like Paul, who said, "Having therefore obtained help of God, I continue unto this day, witnessing both to small and great" (Acts 26:22). Let us also remember that Jesus commanded, "But ye shall receive power, after that the Holy Ghost is come upon you: and ye shall be witnesses unto me both in Jerusalem, and in all Judaea, and in Samaria, and unto the uttermost part of the earth" (Acts 1:8).

Q 70. Where will the saved be during the Great White Throne Judgment?

A I know of no Scripture that clearly tells us where we will be during the Great White Throne Judgment. Jesus said to His own, "Where I am, there ye may be also" (John 14:3). Paul wrote that when Christ comes for His own and we are caught up to meet the Lord in the air, "So shall we ever be with the Lord" (1 Thess. 4:17). It would appear, then, that we Christians will live with Christ wherever He is. He will be the Judge Who sits on the throne at the Great White Throne Judgment (John 5:22), and His people will be with Him.

If we see our lost loved ones at this judgment, we will look at them as God looks at them. He is the One Who will pronounce the sentence upon those who have rejected the Lord Jesus Christ. We, in our new bodies, will be able then to say as the angel said, "Thou art righteous, O Lord, which art, and wast, and shalt be, because thou hast judged thus" (Rev. 16:5). We will be able then to answer Abraham's question, "Shall not the Judge of all the earth do right?" with a resounding "Yes!"

Q 71. Are Americans descendants of any of the twelve tribes of Israel?

A God tells us in 1 Corinthians 10:32 that there are three classes of people in the world: Jews, Gentiles and the Church of Jesus Christ. Commenting on this verse, Alfred Martin wrote, "In the call not to give offense Paul took in the three great ethnic divisions of mankind in God's sight: the Jews, the gentiles . . . and the church. The church is composed of those 'called out' from the other two groups."[149] About 15 million Jews are in the world today. The world has nearly 5.5 billion Gentiles. It has about 100 million members of the Church, the Body of Christ (about 2 percent of the population).

All of the people of the world living today descended from the three sons of Noah and their wives. In Genesis 10:32 we read, "These are the families of the sons of Noah, after their generations, in their nations: and by these were the nations divided in the earth after the flood." Commenting on this fact, The Pilgrim Bible has a note at verse 32 that says, "Every person living has descended from one or the other of Noah's three sons."[150]

Dr. Henry Morris helps us to know the descendants of Noah's three sons:

> Assuming . . . that we can identify fairly well the Semitic Nations (Jews, Arabs, Syrians, Assyrians, Babylonians, Persians, etc.) and the Japhethic Nations (Indo-Europeans), then by process of elimination all others are Hamitic. . . .
>
> Descendants of Ham included the Egyptians and Sumerians, who founded the first two great empires of antiquity, as well as other great nations such as the Phoenicians, Hittites, and Canaanites. The modern African tribes and the Mongol tribes (including today the Chinese and Japanese), as well as the American Indians and the South Sea Islanders, are probably dominantly Hamitic in origin. . . .
>
> In general, however, it has been true throughout history that the Semites have been dominated by religious motivations centered in monotheism (the Jews, the Moslems, the Zoroastrians, etc.). The

Japhethites (especially the Greeks, Romans, and later the other Europeans and the Americans) have stressed science and philosophy in their development. The Hamites (Egyptians, Phoenicians, Sumerians, Orientals, Africans, etc.) have been the great pioneers that opened up the world to settlement, to cultivation, and to technology.[151]

The term "gentiles" was applied especially to the descendants of Japheth. Therefore, most of us in America descended from him, not from Shem as the twelve tribes of Israel did.

Q 72. Is the current wave of horror and occult movies some form of brainwashing, or is this wave just a current fad of young Americans?

A A wave of horror and occult definitely exists in our world. For example, since 1982 violence in children's programming on TV has increased by more than 720 percent. The average child has watched the violent destruction of more than 50,000 persons on TV by the time he is eighteen!

Two movies introduced in the late 1960s and early 1970s, *Night of the Living Dead* and the *Texas Chainsaw Massacre,* made the violent horror movies popular.

Rambo had groups of people killed in more than seventy explosions and had forty-four specific killings, for an average of one death for every 2.1 minutes of the 93-minute film.

Make Them Die Slowly shows twenty-four scenes of barbaric torture, including a scene in which a man slices a woman in two.

This wave of violence is not just a fad; it is an extremely serious problem.

The National Coalition (NCTV) estimated that "25–50 percent of the violence in our society comes from the culture of violence that has been established and gets reinforced every day by violent entertainment."[152]

Dr. Randall P. Harrison wrote in a publication of the American Academy of Pediatrics, "If your eight-year-old watches a lot of TV violence, you can predict that you'll shape him into an aggressive child."[153]

Former U. S. Surgeon General C. Everett Koop reported in 1982 that exposure to violent scenes on television and in the movies is a key factor in stimulating youth violence.[154]

The first TV generation has matured into the most violent in United States history, committing murder, rape and assault at levels 300 to 600 percent higher than any previous generation."[155]

Dr. Thomas Radecki noted in a government hearing, "My conservative estimate . . . would suggest that over a thousand murders every year are the direct result of TV violence. This number could easily be as high as 5,000 or more every year of the 20,000 murders nationwide being directly or indirectly due to TV violence."[156]

The horror and occult movies are not "just a current fad of young Americans," but a serious problem for many people today. Church leaders should help their members to understand the consequences of watching such movies and offer them wholesome alternatives. Parents should supervise what their children view and restrict them from watching horror and occult programs.

It would be well for all of us to join the psalmist as he prayed, "Turn away mine eyes from beholding vanity . . . " (Ps. 119:37), and purpose in our hearts, "I will set no wicked thing before mine eyes . . ." (Ps. 101:3).

Q 73. How do you explain people who claim to have had out-of-body experiences while "clinically dead"?

A Many people claim to have had out-of-body experiences. It is estimated that more than a thousand people a year have encounters with death and live to tell about it. They are revived largely because of our advanced resuscitation techniques. About one-fifth of resuscitated people report to have had some kind of after-life experience.

Dr. Raymond Moody wrote a best-seller in 1975 called *Life after Life,* which details the experiences of about fifty subjects who had been near death or who had been "clinically dead" and then revived. After his book came out, he was swamped with calls from people who offered him more testimonies of that kind of experience. Therefore, he wrote a sequel, *Reflections on Life after Life.* Dr. Moody said that, almost without exception, the life-after-death experience takes away the fear of death.[157]

People do have experiences like these, but they tell us nothing about life after death. The people discussed in Moody's books were not really dead. Their experiences lasted for seconds or minutes at the most. The cells of their bodies did not die, and no evidence exists to prove that brain-wave activity was absent during their experiences. It seems obvious that their brains were active. The reports about life after death by those who did not really die cannot help us to understand life after death. They might tell us some of the feelings of dying people or of people who thought they were dying.

How do we account for these experiences? To answer this question I quote from an excellent book, *Death and the Afterlife,* by Robert A. Morey:

> *While each case must be weighed on its own merits, we submit that the OBE's [Out-of-Body Experiences] related by Moody can be fairly understood as either*
>
> *1. drug experiences,*
> *2. stress and pain responses,*
> *3. hallucinations,*
> *4. dreams, or*
> *5. demonic deceptions.*
>
> *Given the fact that we have only what the patient "feels" happened, there is no scientific way to discern anything beyond the fact that some kind of psychological illusion took place.*
>
> *Last, as Wilson and Weldon point out, "there is a clear parallel to occult phenomena in these experiences." They document that there is nothing "new" in Moody's work. The terminology and interpretations are clearly occultic and stand under the condemnation of Scripture. We are once again confronted with occultic concepts under the guise of a 20th century para-science.*[158]

 74. I have just heard about Dominion Theology. Would you please explain its teachings?

 Dominion Theology, a relatively new movement that began in the 1960s, got its name because it supposedly teaches that Biblical Christianity is to rule, or dominate, every sphere of society. It is also called Reconstructionism because it advocates the reconstruction of society. *Theonomy,* yet another name associated with the movement, teaches that all of society should be brought into obedience to the Mosaic law.

Norman Geisler described it as "a growing movement that threatens both our spiritual and civil liberties."[159]

Charles C. Ryrie spoke of it as "a movement that is misleading many Christians today."[160]

Thomas Ice wrote concerning it, "Reconstructionism cannot be dismissed as a passing, and therefore irrelevant, side-current on the course of evangelical thought. Reconstructionists have garnered support from such disparate groups as old-time fundamentalists, charismatics, and some members of the evangelical intelligentsia."[161]

Its Leaders

The movement has three main leaders: Rousas J. Rushdoony, Gary North and Greg Bahnsen.

Rushdoony was born in New York City in 1916, the son of Armenian immigrants. He was educated at the University of California, the Pacific School of Religion and Valley Christian University. He was a missionary to the Paiute and Shoshone Indians and pastored several Presbyterian churches. He has written about thirty books. He established the Chalcedon Foundation in 1965 in Vallecito, California, where he continues to live, writing and speaking at Christian Reconstruction conferences.

Gary North has a Ph.D. in economics from the University of California—Riverside, and was the editor of *The Journal of Christian Reconstruction* for several years. He now lives in Tyler, Texas, where his Institute for Christian Economics works closely with Geneva Ministries.

Greg Bahnsen was the first student at Westminster Seminary to obtain master of divinity and master of theology degrees simultaneously. He has a Ph.D. from the University of Southern California and taught for some time at Reformed Seminary in Jackson, Mississippi. He currently pastors a small Orthodox Presbyterian church in California and is dean of the graduate school of a local teacher's college.

Other Reconstructionist leaders include David Chilton, a pastor in Placerville, California, and a leading spokesman for Reconstructionists in the field of eschatology; Joseph C. Morecraft III, pastor of Chalcedon Presbyterian Church in Atlanta, Georgia; Gary DeMar, who leads the Institute of Christian Government in Atlanta; James Jordan, pastor of the Reconstructionist church in Tyler, Texas; Ray Sutton, pastor of Good Shepherd Episcopal Church, in Tyler, Texas; George Grant, pastor of Believers Fellowship in Humble, Texas; and Michael Gilstrap, James Michael Peters and Lewis E. Bulkey at Geneva Ministries.[162]

Its Teaching

Reconstructionism strongly opposes dispensationalism. It asserts that God intends the Mosaic law to be in effect throughout history. It is also anti-premillennial. Some Reconstructionists call premillennialism heresy and accuse it of defeatism, of regarding the history of the Church as irrelevant, of draining believers of the motivation to develop the kingdom of God on earth and of being a product of paganism.

Reconstructionism opposes the doctrine of the pretribulational Rapture. It claims that such a view is a dangerous error that teaches God's people to expect defeat instead of victory.

Reconstructionists deny the imminency of the coming of Jesus Christ. They insist He cannot come again for at least a thousand years until the Church has fully developed the kingdom of God on earth.

Reconstructionists believe that God's law applies to every area of life and that all men should obey it. Bahnsen wrote, "The Christian is obligated to keep the whole law of God as a pattern for sanctification and this law is to be enforced by the civil magistrate where and how the stipulations of God so designate."[163]

Reconstructionism takes a postmillennial view of history. It says that man was given a mandate to subdue the earth on behalf of God and thereby establish the kingdom of God on this earth. Because Adam sinned and failed to fulfill the mandate, Satan began to dominate the earth. When Jesus Christ came to earth, He established and restored the Mosaic law as the rule of life for the whole world, defeated Satan and established the kingdom of God. During the present age, Christ is developing the kingdom of God through the faithful obedience of the Church to the dominion mandate. The Church will eventually Christianize the entire world by bringing every nation, institution and culture under the rule of Christ through subjection to the Mosaic law. When the whole world has been brought under Christ's rule, the kingdom of God will have been developed fully and finally on earth. Then Christ will return in His second coming to receive His kingdom.

122

Its Errors

Reconstructionism has a number of problems. It teaches that Christ will not return to earth until after the Millennium. The Bible teaches clearly that Christ will return in His second coming before the Millennium.

It teaches that the kingdom of God has been established in conjunction with the first coming of Christ; that the present age is the kingdom age; that the rule of the kingdom of God is administered without Christ's being physically present on earth and that the Millennium will be present *before,* not *after,* the Second Coming. The Bible teaches that after His second coming, Christ will establish the literal earthly, political, millennial kingdom of God and will be physically present to rule this earth for a thousand years.

However, the book of Revelation predicts that the nations of the world will gather together to battle at Armageddon (Rev. 16:12–16); Christ will come to judge the nations (Rev. 19:11–21); and Christ will rule the world for the thousand-year millennial kingdom (Rev. 20:1–7).

Reconstructionism claims that before the second coming of Christ, world conditions will gradually improve. It also maintains that when Christ returns, He will find the world dominated by the Christian message and the vast majority of mankind converted to true Christianity. By contrast, the Bible teaches that when Christ returns, He will find the world in a chaotic condition of warfare (Joel 3; Zech. 12; 13; 14; Rev. 16:12–16) and the rulers and nations of the earth in a blasphemous state of rebellion against God's rule (Ps. 2:1–3; Rev. 16:9, 11, 21; 19:11–19). Then He will pour out God's wrath upon this seething mass of humanity (Ps. 2:5, 9–12; Joel 3:12–16; Zech. 12:3, 4, 9; 14:3, 12–15; Rev. 19:11–21).

In the book *Dominion Theology: Blessing or Curse?* the authors made the following statements concerning Reconstructionism:

> *Though many of its leaders are brilliant, though its worldview is intriguing, and though its goals are noble, it is just not taught in the Bible. A proper exegesis of God's Word will not produce their most basic ideas. . . .*
>
> *. . . A second major objection to Reconstructionism is that it just does not work. It never has worked in the past, will not work in the present, and will only lead the church astray in the future.*"[164]

Q 75. How does the resurrection spoken of in Matthew 27:52 and 53 fit in if we are to get our new bodies when Christ comes back?

A We Christians will get our new bodies when Christ comes back for His own (1 Cor. 15:51–54; Phil. 3:20, 21). The resurrection spoken of in Matthew 27:52 and 53 refers to the resurrection of the bodies of many saints who came out of the graves immediately after Christ's resurrection. Apparently this resurrection provided further proof of Christ's resurrection. Those resurrected people had died not long before and were known by people still living.

Albert Barnes wrote concerning them, "What became of them after they had entered into the city—whether they again died or ascended to heaven, is not revealed, and conjecture is vain."[165] Matthew Henry commented, "To whom they appeared . . . , whether enemies or friends, in what manner they appeared, how often, what they said and did . . . are secret things which belong not to us. . . ."[166]

Dr. John F. Walvoord wrote concerning their resurrection, "This difficult passage is best explained as an actual resurrection of a token number of saints in keeping with the symbolism of the feast of the firstfruits, when a handful of grain, not just one stalk, was presented to the priest."[167]

Some scholars believe that these people did not die again but were taken directly to Heaven. We can concur with this statement by William L. Pettingill: "How many there were of these, or whether they went back into their graves, or what became of them, this deponent sayeth not, because he knoweth not. It is one of the mysteries that I expect to have cleared up when we get to Heaven."[168]

Q 76. What happened to the men and women who followed God before Jesus came to earth—what group do they belong to, and how did they get to Heaven since Christ hadn't come to earth yet to save them?

A Old Testament believers, both Jews and Gentiles, were saved exactly as New Testament believers were saved: by grace through faith. Jesus Christ died for those who lived before He came into the world, as well as for those who have lived since. Adam and Eve, Noah, Abraham, Moses, David and all the other

Old Testament saints were saved on account of the blood of Jesus. They looked forward to the One Who would come, while those in the New Testament look backward to the One Who came. In God's plan of redemption, Jesus Christ was reckoned as "the Lamb slain from the foundation of the world" (Rev. 13:8).

Speaking of Jesus Christ, God said, "Whom God hath set forth to be a propitiation through faith in his blood, to declare his righteousness for the remission of sins that are past, through the forbearance of God" (Rom. 3:25). Hebrews 9:15 teaches that Christ died "for the redemption of the transgressions that were under the first testament. . . ."

The people saved in the Old Testament were Jews and Gentiles. They did not belong to the Church because it did not start until Pentecost, fifty days after the resurrection of Christ.

Q 77. What is the difference between the midtribulation Rapture belief and the pre-wrath Rapture belief?

A I have been a Christian for about fifty years, and all those years I have loved to study prophecy and to preach prophetic messages. Until 1990 I had known of a number of positions concerning the Rapture:

Partial Rapture, which teaches that only those who are faithful to the Lord and watching for Him will be caught up before the Tribulation.

Midtribulation Rapture, which teaches that the Church will endure the first half of the Tribulation and will be raptured in the middle of the Tribulation.

Posttribulation Rapture, which teaches that the Church must pass through the Tribulation and then will be translated at the close.

Pretribulation Rapture, which teaches that Christ will rapture true believers before the tribulation period.

I have always believed and preached that Christ will come for His Church before the Tribulation. I have never read anything or heard anything that has caused me to change my thinking concerning this subject.

In 1990 a new theory, called the *Pre-wrath Rapture,*[169] surfaced. It teaches these principles:

1. The rapture of the church will occur immediately prior to the beginning of the Day of the Lord.
2. The Day of the Lord commences sometime within the second half of the seventieth week.
3. The cosmic disturbances associated with the sixth seal will signal the approach of the Day of the Lord.
4. The Day of the Lord will begin with the opening of the seventh seal (Rev. 8:1).

Marvin Rosenthal, for about sixteen years the director of the Friends of Israel Gospel Ministry, presented this new theory in his book *The Pre-wrath Rapture of the Church*. Because of his change in thinking, he was not permitted to remain at the mission. In May of 1989 he started a new ministry as director of Zion's Hope, a faith mission in Orlando, Florida.

After reading his book, I can repeat what I stated above: I have never read anything or heard anything that has caused me to change my thinking concerning this subject (the pretribulation Rapture).

Rosenthal wrote, "Within two years many men will be teaching the pre-wrath Rapture. Within five years it will be a recognized position. And, if God pleases, within fifteen years it will become a major position of the believing church—if God gives that many years."[170]

Perhaps within two years men will teach the pre-wrath Rapture, and perhaps within five years it will be a recognized position. Nevertheless, God will not be pleased for it to become a major position of the Church, because it is not the position of the Word of God.

Rosenthal takes the position that God's wrath on the earth will not start until the Day of the Lord after the six seals of Revelation 6 and after cosmic disturbances. He further states that Christ will rapture the Church just before the beginning of wrath, since 1 Thessalonians 5:9 states that believers of this age are not appointed to wrath.

He wrote, "Wrath is restricted to the latter part of the seventieth week, specifically the Day of the Lord period,"[171] and "God's wrath does not start until the opening of the seventh seal."[172]

Luke 21:23 says, "But woe unto them that are with child, and to them that give suck, in those days! for there shall be great distress in the land, and wrath upon this people." This verse parallels Matthew 24:19–22. Matthew referred to this time as one that has "great tribulation" (v. 21). Luke taught there will be wrath during the time Matthew describes as having "great tribulation."

Paul S. Karleen evaluated Rosenthal's book in *The Pre-wrath*

Rapture of the Church: Is It Biblical? Karleen wrote, "The text of Luke is clear. There is wrath during the period where the author of *Pre-Wrath* places the Tribulation, during the period where he places the six seals, before the seventh seal, before his cosmic disturbances, before where he places the Rapture, and before his Day of the Lord starts—all times when he says there cannot be wrath."[173]

When we read the sixth chapter of Revelation, we find the Antichrist appearing (vv. 1, 2), war (vv. 3, 4), famine (vv. 5, 6), one-fourth of the people killed (vv. 7, 8), martyrs (vv. 9–11) and cosmic disturbances. To say no wrath appears until the seventh seal (Rev. 8:1) is more than I can believe.

In his article "The Rapture of the Church," Dr. Renald Showers wrote, "The first four seals [of Revelation 6] will take place during the first half of the 70th week, those seals will involve a great future outpouring of God's wrath upon the earth, and the Church will be removed from the earth before that outpouring of God's wrath upon the earth. It must be concluded, therefore, that the Church will be removed from the earth before the first half of the 70th week."[174]

Rosenthal's book has a few problems that I will mention briefly.

First, he believes Christians will have to endure the persecution of the Antichrist. If that is so, Christians must look for Antichrist, not Christ. They can no longer expect Christ at any moment. Imminency has been lost and with it the "blessed hope." If the Church must remain on the earth to face Antichrist, the Christians would refuse to take his mark and would be put to death (Rev. 13:7, 15–18).

Second, he states that the multitude of Revelation 7 is the "true Church."[175]

Third, he claims that no significant period of time exists between the Rapture and the Day of the Lord.[176]

Fourth, he believes that the apostasy in 2 Thessalonians 2:3 refers to Jews.[177]

Fifth, he says the restrainer of 2 Thessalonians 2 is the archangel Michael.[178]

At the beginning of his book he wrote, "If I am wrong, ten thousand angels arguing my cause would not make it right, and I will have played the fool."[179] At the close of his book he made the following statements, and he is not wrong here: "Apart from some notable exceptions, at the present hour the church is splintered, polarized, carnal, materialistic, humanistic, and impotent. The world is *burning,* and the church is *fiddling.*"[180]

Q 78. What happens to a Christian who commits suicide?

A Suicide, an extremely old practice, is a tragic form of death that greatly shocks and grieves the loved ones left behind.

Suicide is rising sharply among young people and is topped only by accidental death as the most common cause of death in that age group. Hungary has the highest overall suicide rate in the world—33.1 suicides per 100,000 people. Here are several other countries' statistics:

- Czechoslovakia—24.5 per 100,000
- Austria—22.3 per 100,000
- Sweden—22.0 per 100,000
- The United States—11.7 per 100,000

The World Health Organization estimates that at least 1,000 persons commit suicide every day in the world and that more than 1.5 million suicides occur annually. For every "successful" suicide, at least eight to ten attempts are made.

Every minute at least one person in the U.S. tries to kill himself. About 30,000 people commit suicide each year in the U.S.A.

The Bible mentions at least six people who committed suicide:
Samson (Judges 16:29, 30);
King Saul (1 Sam. 31:4, 5);
King Saul's armor bearer (1 Sam. 31:5);
Ahithophel (2 Sam. 17:23);
Zimri (1 Kings 16:18);
Judas (Matt. 27:5).

It is possible for a Christian to commit suicide. I have talked to Christians who have tried to commit suicide and others who have thought about it. Of course, suicide is a sin, a violation of both law and grace, but it is not the unpardonable sin, as some people believe. No Christian (or any other person) should take his own life. If a Christian commits suicide, he will meet the Lord ashamed and will suffer loss at the Judgment Seat of Christ (1 Cor. 3:15; 1 John 2:28).

He will not lose his salvation, because when God saves a person, He gives that person eternal life, and that person will never perish (John 10:27–29). Some people have the impression that if a Christian sins and dies before he confesses his sin, he will be lost. But the Bible does not teach that idea. God promised in 1 John 1:9: "If we confess our sins, he is faithful and just to forgive us our sins, and to cleanse us from all unrighteousness."

Some believers claim that if a sin is unconfessed, it is also unforgiven. But this principle refers to governmental or disciplinary forgiveness, and it does not touch the question of a Christian's eternal salvation in any way.

In his book *Why Me, Lord?* Paul W. Powell discussed suicide and salvation.

> *Our salvation is not based on the way we die. It is determined by our relationship with Jesus Christ. If we are trusting Christ as our Saviour when we die, we are saved. If not, we are lost (John 3:16–18). The manner of our death does not enter into the picture.*

> *It is my feeling that a person who commits suicide is temporarily insane. Since the instinct of self-preservation is usually man's strongest, to take one's life is an irrational deed. Such a person is to be pitied and not condemned. After all, we do not know how many valiant battles the person may have fought before he lost that one particular battle. Is it fair that all the good acts and impulses of such a person should be forgotten and blotted out by one final tragic act? Each one of us, probably, has a final breaking point. Life puts far more pressure on some of us than it does on others. Some people have more stamina than others. So our reaction to suicide should be one of love and pity, not condemnation.*

> *Remember that our salvation depends on our relationship with Christ. He offers us eternal salvation. Not even suicide can change that.*[181]

Q 79. Will a time come when people will try to commit suicide and will be unable to die?

A Revelation 9:1–6 tells us that people will want to die but that they will be unable to do so. According to this Scripture passage, for a five-month period during the coming Tribulation, men will "seek death and shall not find it; and shall desire to die, and death shall flee from them" (v. 6). "Locusts" in this passage refers to demonic creatures that will come from the bottomless pit (the Abyss) and torment men for five months. Their torment will be as the torment of a scorpion when it strikes a man. The sting of a natural scorpion usually is not fatal, but it produces perhaps the most intense pain that any creature can inflict on the human body. These creatures from the pit will produce such agony that men will seek death, but death will flee from them.

John Phillips wrote about what will happen: "Imagine a world in which men court death, attempt suicide, expose themselves to the reaper's scythe, chase after him with all their might, only to find that, for once, he cannot be found! These tormented men cannot die, yet they are in anguish beyond words to describe. It is hell on earth."[182]

I read the story of a man who tried to commit suicide by jumping off a platform in front of a subway train. He jumped from the platform, and the train hit him and knocked him back to the platform without any injury. I thought of Revelation 9:1–6 when I read the report in the newspaper.

I also read in the newspaper this story:

London hairdresser Carl Moss, 23, depressed by money problems and a break with his girlfriend, tried to commit suicide six times in one night but failed every time, police told a court at Chichester.

After drinking half a bottle of gin to get his courage up, Moss walked into the sea at nearby Worthing, but lost his nerve after the water reached his chest.

He returned to his hairdressing shop and wired up a metal chair and twice tried to electrocute himself, but each time he threw the switch, a fuse blew.

Then he broke a mirror and cut his wrists, but the cuts were ineffective. He tried to hang himself from a stair rail, but the knot came loose.

In a final bid, Moss piled up furniture and cushions and set them on fire hoping the smoke would suffocate him. But the fire got too hot and he climbed out of a window and went to the Samaritans, a non-profit organization dedicated to helping people with problems.[183]

Speaking of the tormented men in the coming tribulation period, Dr. Henry Morris said, "One can hope that some of these tormented men and women will finally break down and repent and call on God for forgiveness and salvation. God's longsuffering desire for their repentance (II Pet. 3:9) is probably the very reason He will not allow them to die during this unspeakable five months."[184]

Q 80. What does the New Age movement teach?

A The New Age movement is a loose organization of people who believe that the world has entered the Aquarian Age when peace on earth and one-world government will rule. They reject Judeo-Christian values and the Bible in favor of Oriental philosophies and religion. Among them may be found environmentalists, nuclear-freeze proponents, Marxist-socialist utopians, mind-control advocates, ESP cultists, spiritists, witchcraft practitioners, magical rite users, famous entertainers, actors, authors, scientists, researchers and people from all levels of society.

Its leaders include Shirley MacLaine; Ruth Montgomery; Marilyn Ferguson; Werner Erhard, founder of EST (Erhard Seminars Training); Fritjof Capra, a physicist who authored the New Age texts *The Tao of Physics* and *The Turning Point;* Benjamin Creme, the self-proclaimed forerunner of a New Age guru, Maitreya; Robert Muller, recently retired Assistant to the Secretary General of the United Nations; Alice Bailey; J. Z. Knight, a New Age channeler; and David Spangler.

According to Marilyn McGuire, executive director of the New Age Publishing and Retailing Alliance, the U.S. has about 2,500 occult bookstores and more than 3,000 publishers of occult books and journals. Sales of New Age books in particular are estimated at $1 billion a year.[185]

In his book *The New Age Cult,* the late Walter Martin gave ten key doctrines of the New Age movement. I want to condense them to help us see what the New Agers believe. The quotes come from their own writings.

Concerning God

In a sense there is no such thing as God, God does not exist. And in another sense, there is nothing else but God—only God exists. . . . All is God. And because all is God, there is no God.[186]

Concerning the Trinity

Eternal Thought is one; in essence it is two—Intelligence and Force; and when they breathe, a child is born; this child is Love.

And thus the Triune God stands forth, whom men call Father-Mother-Child.[187]

Concerning Jesus Christ

People have been led to leave the churches in large numbers because the churches have presented a picture of the Christ impossible for the majority of thinking people today to accept— as the one and only Son of God, sacrificed by His Loving Father to save Humanity from the results of its sins; as a Blood Sacrifice straight out of the old and outworn Jewish Dispensation; as the unique revealer of God's nature, once and forever, never to be enlarged and expanded as man himself grows in awareness and ability to receive other revelations of that Divine nature; and as waiting in some mythical and unattractive Heaven until the end of the world, when He will return in a cloud of glory to the sound of Angels' trumpets, and descending from these clouds, inherit His Kingdom.

The majority of thinking people today have rejected this view. . . .[188]

Concerning Salvation

Jesus: "How simple is salvation! All it says is what was never true (i.e., sin and its punishment) is not true now, and never will be. The impossible has not occurred, and can have no effects. And that is all."[189]

Concerning the Atonement

God does not believe in retribution. His Mind does not create that way. He does not hold your "evil" deeds against you. Is it likely that He would hold them against me? . . .

Sacrifice is a notion totally unknown to God. It arises solely from fear, and frightened people can be vicious. Sacrificing in any way is a violation of my injunction that you should be merciful even as your Father in Heaven is merciful.[190]

Concerning Heaven, Hell and the Last Judgment

Jesus: "My brother, man, your thoughts are wrong; your heaven is not far away; and it is not a place of metes and bounds, is not a country to be reached; it is a state of mind.

God never made a heaven for man; he never made a hell; we are creators and we make our own.

Now, cease to seek for heaven in the sky; just open up the windows of your heart, and, like a flood of light, a heaven will come and bring a boundless joy; then toil will be no cruel task."[191]

Those who believe in a hell and assign themselves to it through their belief can indeed experience one, but certainly in nothing like eternal terms.[192]

Jesus: "The Last Judgment is one of the most threatening ideas in your thinking. This is because you do not understand it. Judgment is not an attribute of God. It was brought into being only after the separation (i.e., man's fall into delusion), when it became one of the many learning devices to be built into the overall plan. . . ."[193]

Concerning Demonic Powers

It is important to see that Lucifer, as I am using this term, describes an angel, a being, a great and mighty planetary consciousness. It does not describe that popular thought-form of Satan who seeks to lead man down a path of sin and wrongdoing. That is a human creation, and yet it is a creation that has some validity but represents the collective thought-form of all those negative energies which man has built up and created.

Man is his own Satan just as man is his own salvation.[194]

Concerning the Second Coming of Christ

In a very real sense, Findhorn (a New Age community in Scotland) represents the Second Coming. Any individual, any center, who so embodies the new that it becomes a magnetic source to draw the new out of the rest of the world, embodies the Second Coming.[195]

Concerning Reincarnation

This doctrine will be one of the keynotes of the new world religion, as well as the clarifying agent for a better understanding of world affairs. When Christ was here, in person, before . . . He told them to "Be ye therefore perfect even as your Father which is in Heaven is perfect" (Matt. 5:48).

This time, He will teach men the method whereby this possibility can become accomplished fact—through the constant return of the incarnating soul to the school of life on Earth, there to undergo the perfection process of which He was the outstanding example. That is the meaning and teaching of reincarnation.[196]

Concerning the New Age

The Aquarian Age is preeminently a spiritual age, and the spiritual side of the great lessons that Jesus gave to the world may now be comprehended by multitudes of people, for the many are now coming into an advanced stage of spiritual consciousness. . . .[197]

> *As we enter into the New Age, what we are entering into is a cycle, a period of time, a period of unfoldment when truly humanity is the world initiate, the world saviour, and ultimately it is upon the shoulders of humanity that the future and the translation for the entry into light of this planet rest.*[198]

Christians are being influenced by the New Age movement because they do not study the Word of God. We need to search the Scriptures daily to see what God says, and then we need to obey the Word of God. We need to be informed about the New Age. We conclude with Walter Martin's challenge:

> *In dealing with the New Age Cult, we are in reality dealing with spiritual warfare against the forces of darkness, and we are told by God to put on the whole armor of heaven so that we will be able to withstand the forces of Satan (Eph. 6:11).*

> *There is no substitute in this conflict for knowledge of the Word of God and the proper use of the sword of the Spirit and the shield of faith to deflect all the flaming arrows of the evil one. The forces arrayed against us are great, the stakes are high: the souls of millions of people. But the promise of God stands sure, we can*

"overcome them: because greater is he that is in you, than he that is in the world" (I John 4:4).[199]

Q 81. Do other civilizations exist in other solar systems?

A Not the slightest evidence exists, either Biblical or scientific, that men like us inhabit other planets or star systems. For life to exist, water must abound. Little, if any, water exists on the moon, Mars, Venus or the other planets. The temperatures on other planets are either too hot or too cold for human life.

Also, many complex chemicals must be present to support life processes. No evidence indicates that such a planet with an atmosphere like ours exists anywhere else in the universe.

God's Word clearly teaches that man is to inhabit this earth. "The heaven, even the heavens, are the LORD'S: but the earth hath he given to the children of men" (Ps. 115:16). God "hath made of one blood all nations of men for to dwell on all the face of the earth, and hath determined the times before appointed, and the bounds of their habitation" (Acts 17:26).

Jesus Christ came to this earth, not to any other of the billions of heavenly bodies, to die for our sins and provide salvation for us. "This is a faithful saying, and worthy of all acceptation, that Christ Jesus came into the world to save sinners; of whom I am chief" (1 Tim. 1:15). It seems unthinkable that God would send His Son to millions of other planets to die. God had only one Son, and He sent Him to the one planet where there is human life.

Dr. Henry Morris wrote, "Thus, although it is all but certain that no other man-like creatures inhabit other worlds, it is true that in God's universe, and possibly on the stars themselves, there exists a vast host of intelligent and powerful beings, the angels of God."[200]

Q 82. When will the Old Testament saints be raised from the dead?

A Many prophetic scholars say the Old Testament saints will be raised from the dead at the Rapture. For example, the *Scofield Reference Bible* note says, ". . . the saints of the O.T. and church ages meeting Him in the air (1 Thess. 4:16, 17); while the martyrs of the tribulation . . . are raised at the end of the tribulation. . . ."[201] Some of these scholars teach that since the redemption of Israel depends on the work of Christ, as does the redemption of the Church saints, Old Testament saints are "in Christ" and will be resurrected at the same time. Another note in the Scofield Bible says, "Not church saints only, but all bodies of the saved, of whatever dispensation, are included in the first resurrection . . . as here [in I Thess. 4:13–18] described, but it is peculiarly the 'blessed hope' of the church. . . ."[202]

The New Scofield Reference Bible (NSRB) presents another view. It suggests "that it is more harmonious with the O.T. Scriptures to include the O.T. believers with those who rise after the tribulation (Rev. 20:4–6), because both Isaiah and Daniel mention the resurrection of O.T. saints as taking place following a time of great trouble (Isa. 26:16–21; Dan. 12:1–3)."[203] The notes on page 1292 mention only the church in connection with 1 Thessalonians 4:13–18. The notes on page 918 teach that the resurrection in view in Daniel 12:2 "will occur after the tribulation and concerns O.T. believers—not the Church, which will be translated before the tribulation."

John L. Benson made the following comments concerning the resurrection of Old Testament saints:

> *Isaiah 26:18 describes the tribulation; Isaiah 26:19 speaks of Israel's resurrection following the tribulation. . . . [Daniel spoke of] "a time of trouble, such as never was since there was a nation even to that same time." At that time Daniel's people—the Jews— will be delivered; and at that time "many of them that sleep in the dust of the earth shall awake" (verse 2). Can anything be plainer? The resurrection of Israel will follow tribulation woes.*[204]

 Q 83. Are all saved people the elect of God, or are there special provisions to become the elect?

A The verb "to choose" or "to elect" *(eklego; eklegomai)* is found twenty-one times in the New Testament.

- Eight times it refers to Christ's choosing or electing His disciples (Luke 6:13; John 6:70; 13:18; 15:16 [twice]; 15:19; Acts 1:2, 24).

- Six times it does not pertain to salvation (Luke 10:42; 14:7; Acts 6:5; 15:7, 22, 25).
- Seven times it refers to men and women as the objects of election to eternal life (Mark 13:20; Acts 13:17; 1 Cor. 1:27 [twice], 28; Eph. 1:4; James 2:5).

The noun "elect" *(eklektos)* is used twenty-three times in the New Testament.

- Three times it speaks of Christ as the "elect" one (Luke 23:35; 1 Pet. 2:4, 6).
- One time it refers to angels (1 Tim. 5:21).
- One time it refers to Rufus, chosen in the Lord (Rom. 16:13).
- Eighteen times it is used of men and women as God's "elect," those chosen to eternal life (Matt. 20:16; 22:14; 24:22, 24, 31; Mark 13:20, 22, 27; Luke 18:7; Rom. 8:33; Col. 3:12; 2 Tim. 2:10; Titus 1:1; 1 Pet. 1:2; 2:9; 2 John 1, 13; Rev. 17:14).

Seven times the Bible uses a word that means "election" *(ekloge)*. Each time, it refers to salvation (Acts 9:15; Rom. 9:11; 11:5, 7, 28; 1 Thess. 1:4; 2 Pet. 1:10).

Election means "to choose" or "to pick." God is the One Who chooses; believers are the chosen ones. "According as he hath chosen us in him before the foundation of the world" (Eph 1:4). God chose people before they actually lived on earth, before they personally received Jesus Christ as Savior, before their parents were born, before Christ died on the cross and even before He created the universe.

God chose His own "in Him"; namely, in Jesus Christ. Salvation has always been in and through Him. God could not choose anyone apart from the atoning sacrifice of the Lord Jesus Christ. It is His merit, not ours, that makes our election possible.

Bishop J. C. Ryle is helpful in our understanding of election:

Election to eternal life is a truth of Scripture which we must receive humbly, and believe implicitly. Why the Lord Jesus calls some and does not call others, quickens whom He will, and leaves others alone in their sins, these are deep things which we cannot explain. Let it suffice us to know it is a fact. God must begin the work of grace in a man's heart, or else a man will never be saved. Christ must first choose us and call us by His Spirit, or else we shall never choose Christ. Beyond doubt, if not saved, we shall have none to blame but ourselves. But if saved, we shall certainly trace up the beginning of our salvation, to the choosing grace of Christ.

Our song to all eternity will be that which fell from the lips of Jonah: "Salvation is of the Lord" (Jonah 2:9).

Election is always to sanctification. Those whom Christ chooses out of mankind, He chooses not only that they may be saved, but that they may bear fruit, and fruit that can be seen. All other election beside this is a mere vain delusion, and a miserable invention of man. . . . Where there is no visible fruit of sanctification, we may be sure there is no election.[205]

C. Samuel Storms wrote:

Like everything else that God does, election has a goal. The immediate goal of election is the salvation of those chosen. . . . Of course, this does not mean that the eternal destiny of individuals is the only objective in election. . . .

But the will of God for His elect does not terminate when they come to saving faith in Jesus Christ. Paul makes it clear that God the Father chose us in Christ in order that we should be holy and blameless in His glorious presence (Eph. 1:4). The Apostle Peter likewise insists that God has chosen a people in order that they might "obey" Jesus Christ (1 Pet. 1:1–2; see also 1 Pet. 2:9, Rom. 8:28). But surely the ultimate or final good of God's electing love is God's own glory. He chose us that we should be both justified and sanctified, all of which is designed to redound to "the praise of the glory of His grace" (Eph. 1:6, 12, 14; cf. Rom. 9:17–23).[206]

Warren W. Wiersbe wrote: "In the Bible, election is always *unto* something. It is a privilege that carries a great responsibility."[207]

I have found seven reasons why God chooses people.
1. He chooses people in order to save some (John 3:16; Acts 13:48; 2 Thess. 2:13; 2 Tim. 1:9).
2. He chooses people so that they will be holy and blameless (Eph. 1:4; Col. 3:12, 13; 1 Pet. 1:15, 16).
"The real purpose of God's elective grace is not 'pie in the sky by and by,' but has to do with a separated life here and now (cf. Rom 8:29). Holiness is the positive side of a Christlike life (Heb 12:14), separated from all evil courses and connections."[208]

138

3. He chooses people so that they will live humbly before Him (1 Cor. 12:26–31).
4. He chooses people so that they will live fruitful lives (John 15:16).
5. He chooses people so that they will show forth His praises (1 Pet. 2:9).
6. He chooses people so that they might be to the praise of His glory (Eph. 1:4–14).
7. He chooses people so that they will be conformed to the image of Christ (Rom. 8:28, 29).

Dr. Henry Morris wrote the following discussion of God's sovereignty and man's responsibility:

It is clear, therefore, that every person, without exception, can be saved if he wants to be, by coming in simple faith to accept Jesus Christ as his personal Lord and Saviour. And yet, we also read that Jesus said, "No man can come to me except the Father which hath sent me draw him" (John 6:44). He also said, "Ye have not chosen me, but I have chosen you" (John 15:16). When the gospel was preached, it was said that "As many as were ordained to eternal life believed" (Acts 13:48).

A person who has accepted Christ and been born again through faith in Him knows that he has done so voluntarily. Yet, when he reflects more carefully, he sees that many different circumstances— his family background, his friends, his personal difficulties, the messages and testimonies he has heard, the Scriptures he has read—have all contributed to the decision.

Then he begins to see that God was working in his life long before he came to the actual point of decision. It's as though he had come to a single great doorway in an endless wall, over which was inscribed the words: "By me, if any man enter in, he shall be saved" (John 10:9). And so, he voluntarily accepts the invitation and enters the door.

To his astonished gratitude, he finds himself in a magnificent paradise stretching as far as he can see. Glancing back at the gateway through which he had entered, he is amazed that there is no gate to be seen at all. Instead, on the wall are emblazoned the words: "Chosen in him before the foundation of the world" (Eph. 1:4).

Although we cannot, in our present finite understanding, completely resolve the mystery surrounding God's "determinate counsel and foreknowledge" (Acts 2:23), we may nevertheless derive great joy and strength from His assurance that we who have acknowledged His Son as Saviour and Lord have been "predestinated according to the purpose of him who worketh all things after the counsel of his own will" (Eph. 1:11).

For those who are not yet believing Christians, on the other hand, the issue remains one of human responsibility—either to live a life of absolute holiness and sinless perfection from birth to death (as did Jesus Christ), or else to come in repentant faith to that One who died for man's sin and was raised for his justification. For it is written that "whosoever believeth in him should not perish, but have eternal life" (John 3:15).[209]

Q 84. Should a Christian join a local church? Is it possible to be a Christian without joining a church?

A In 1988, religious groups in the U.S.A. had about 142,799,622 members. Statistics indicate that 90 percent of all church members in America are unsaved and that up to 50 percent of the members of fundamental churches in America are unsaved. Nevertheless, every Christian should belong to a Bible-preaching local church for four main reasons.

First, the Bible emphasizes local churches. The word "church" appears 115 times in the New Testament, and in at least 95 of these uses, the word refers to local churches. A few times the word refers to the mystical Body of Christ. Surely, if God gives the local church this kind of prominence, we cannot afford to think lightly of it. We should give careful attention to what He says about the local church.

Second, God ordained local churches to fulfill the Great Commission. The Great Commission was given to the apostles (Matt. 28:16–20; Acts 1:2, 8). The apostles organized the first local church under the guidance of the Holy Spirit (Acts 2:41, 42), and people from this church planted other churches (Acts 8:1–17). Paul's missionary work began in a local church (Acts 13:1, 2), and he reported to this same church (Acts 14:26, 27). Paul wrote his epistles to local churches, and Jesus addressed His last words to the local churches (Rev 1:11; 2; 3).

Third, local churches are the channels of Christian service. We are saved to serve. In his book *Should I Join a Church?* Arnold T. Olson explained the importance of the church as a place of service:

The task of making Christ known is an endless one. It is beyond the ability of a single individual. It involves many things:

• The training of workers;
• The printing of Bibles and Bible literature;
• The sending forth of workers;
• The erecting and maintenance of church buildings;
• The establishment of new gospel centers and congregations.

In the local congregation there is the teaching of the child, the guidance of the youth, the strengthening of the adult, the ministry to the sick, the evangelizing of the lost, the confirming of the young believer.

There is all of this and much more. No one person can do all of it. To each is given a small part in the great program. I thus pool my efforts with those of the many—teaching but a few, supporting financially in part, praying daily in the closet and weekly in the fellowship, singing one part in the four-part harmony, giving a word of testimony as part of the message going around the world. Dedicated to the task of making Christ known, I am determined to reach as many as possible. This I do through my membership in my church.

My tithe might not be adequate to support fully a single missionary, publish a single Bible, finance a single translation, build one Sunday School room, erect a church building. But by adding mine to that of the many others these tasks can be accomplished. My testimony in the community can reach, at best, just a few but by joining with the others, I can make an impact for Christ which will be felt there and around the world.[210]

Fourth, New Testament local churches were organized and had members. A. H. Strong wrote:

Organization may exist without knowledge of writing, without written records, lists of members, or formal choice of officers. These last are the proofs, reminders and helps of organization, but they are not essential to it. It is however not merely informal, but formal, organization in the church, to which the New Testament bears witness.[211]

Local churches had regular meetings (Acts 20:7; Heb. 10:25), officers were elected or appointed (Phil. 1:1), letters of recommendation were sent (Acts 18:27), a register of widows was kept (1 Tim. 5:9), discipline was exercised (1 Cor. 5), believers had a right to vote (Acts 6:5), and the ordinances were administered (Acts 2:42).

For a church to own property, maintain a treasury, receive tax-exempt funds, maintain real estate, call a pastor or send out missionaries, church membership is necessary.

I have heard many people say, "The New Testament never refers to membership in a local church, but only to membership in the mystical Church." The best answer to this statement, in my opinion, has been given by the late Dr. Kenneth H. Good in his booklet *Why Every Christian Should Be a Member of a Local Church*. He wrote:

142

Now, in order to answer the above objection, we refer to I Cor. 1:2, where we observe that the letter of Paul was written primarily to a local church in Corinth. In 3:16, 17, this church is called a temple of God. In 12:27, still referring to the same local church, Paul says, "Now ye are the body of Christ, and members in particular." In the Greek text there is no definite article preceding the word "body." It should read, "Now ye are a body of Christ, and members in particular." John Nelson Darby translates it "Now ye are Christ's body, and members in particular." That is, a local church is not only a temple in which God dwells, it is also a body of which Christ is the Head. This body is made up of individual members, *who are called by that term in the Word of God. We never need to be apologetic about calling ourselves* members *of a local church as though the term were of human invention and unspiritual. . . .*

Those who framed our church covenant understood that to be the meaning of I Cor. 12:27, when they inscribed: "Having been brought, as we trust, by divine grace to embrace the Lord Jesus Christ as our Saviour, and having been baptized, upon the confession of our faith, in the Name of the Father, the Son, and the Holy Spirit, we do now most solemnly enter into covenant with one another as one body in Christ."[212]

Although it is extremely important for you to join a church, don't assume that just any church will do. The church you join should preach and teach all of the Bible. It should believe and teach that the Bible is verbally inspired; that Jesus Christ is the sinless, virgin-born Son of God; that He died for our sins and rose again for our justification; that one day He is going to return; that He is the only One Who can save; that we are saved through faith in the shed blood of Christ. The church you join should be separated from other churches and denominations that do not preach the Word of God. For example, it should in no way affiliate with the National Council of Churches or the World Council of Churches.

So we conclude that every believer should join a Bible-believing, Bible-teaching church. But can a person be a Christian if he does not belong to a local church? Yes, it is possible, but it is something like being

A student who will not go to school;
A soldier who will not join an army;

A citizen who does not pay taxes or vote;
A salesman without any customers;
An explorer with no base camp;
A seaman on a ship without a crew;
A businessman on a deserted island;
An author without readers;
A tuba player without an orchestra;
A parent without a family;
A football player without a team;
A politician who is a hermit;
A scientist who does not share his findings;
A bee without a hive.

—Wesleyan Christian Advocate[213]

Q 85. Does God ever give up on anyone?

A I have often heard this saying: "As long as there is life, there is hope." The Bible teaches otherwise. Sometimes God gives men up, as we see in Romans 1:24–28. Three times in this passage we read, "God also gave them up . . . God gave them up . . . God gave them over . . ." (vv. 24, 26, 28). Dr. S. Lewis Johnson, Jr., in his article in *Bibliotheca Sacra,* "God Gave Them Up," wrote:

> *The meaning is not simply that God withdrew from the wicked the restraining force of His providence and common grace . . . but that He positively gave men over to the judgment of "more intensified and aggravated cultivation of the lust of their own hearts with the result that they reap for themselves a correspondingly greater toll of retributive vengeance."*[214]

Johnson concluded, "One must conclude from Romans 1:24, 26, and 28 that retributive justice is an attribute of the living God and a necessary feature of His actions toward unbelieving man. To the question, 'Can God really give man up to judgment?' this passage provides a resounding 'yes' answer."[215]

Romans 1:24, 26 and 28 name three things that God gives man up to:

144

God gives men up to uncleanness ". . . to dishonour their own bodies between themselves" (v. 24).

God gives men up ". . . unto vile affections" (v. 26).

God gives men over ". . . to a reprobate mind" (v. 28).

God gives men up, body, soul and spirit, but only when they give God up. Dr. A. T. Robertson said concerning these three times when God gives men up, "The words sound to us like clods on the coffin as God leaves men to work out their own wicked will."[216]

Someone has written: "Better any punishment than that God shall leave us alone, or give us up." Someone else has said, "The most dreadful fate for any man is for God to say to him, 'Thy will be done.'"

In John 12:37–40 we read:

But though he had done so many miracles before them, yet they believed not on him: That the saying of Esaias the prophet might be fulfilled, which he spake, Lord, who hath believed our report? and to whom hath the arm of the Lord been revealed? Therefore they could not believe, because that Esaias said again, He hath blinded their eyes, and hardened their heart; that they should not see with their eyes, nor understand with their heart, and be converted, and I should heal them.

Notice again verses 37 and 39: "They believed not on him. . . . Therefore they could not believe." They would not believe on Him, and then they could not believe on Him. Arthur W. Pink commented on this fact when he wrote, "They *would not* believe; in consequence they *could not* believe. The harvest was past, the summer was ended, and they were not saved. But the fault was entirely theirs, and now they must suffer the just consequences of their wickedness."[217]

Bishop J. C. Ryle commented on this passage:

"They could not," is literally, "they were not able." It precisely describes the moral inability of a thoroughly hardened and wicked man to believe. He is thoroughly under the mastery of a hardened and seared conscience, and has, as it were, lost the power of believing.

They had no will to believe, and so they had no power. They could have believed if they would, but they would not, and so they could not.[218]

J. Vernon McGee gave this warning: "My friend, the most dangerous thing in the world is to hear the gospel and then turn your back on it. If you just go on listening and do not accept it and act upon it, there comes the time when you cannot hear and you cannot see. God is God, and it is He who has the final word."[219]

One of the most frightening passages in the Word of God is Proverbs 1:24–32, which records the fact that God calls, and people refuse. He stretches out His hand, and no man regards it. People set at naught (disregard) His counsel; they will not heed His reproof; they hate His knowledge; they do not choose the fear of the Lord. God says He will laugh at their calamity, mock when their fear comes and will not answer them when they call. He then warns, "Therefore shall they eat of the fruit of their own way, and be filled with their own devices. For the turning away of the simple shall slay them, and the prosperity of fools shall destroy them" (vv. 31, 32).

Dr. Harry Ironside related how the Spirit of God used this passage of Scripture in his life:

> *These words must ever possess a tender and precious interest for the writer. It was through having learned them as a lad in the Sunday-school that I was, when fourteen years of age, truly awakened by the Spirit of God to see the awful result of rejecting the call of the gospel. Unable to shake off the vivid impression of God's righteous wrath if I longer refused His grace, I fell down before Him confessing myself a lost, undone sinner, and found in John 3:16 the solace my conscience needed: "For God so loved the world, that He gave His only begotten Son, that whosoever believeth in Him should not perish, but have everlasting life." It was a night to be remembered forever![220]*

My prayer for any unbelieving reader is that the Spirit of God will awaken you to see the awful result of rejecting the call of the gospel and that you will, like Ironside, fall down before the Lord, confess yourself a lost, undone sinner and find in John 3:16 the solace your conscience needs. Give up to God—don't cause God to give up on you.

 86. If a person claims to be a child of God and God does not chasten him when he sins, is he really saved?

A The Bible teaches clearly that God chastens His children. Chastening means child training, instruction and discipline. "For whom the Lord loveth he chasteneth, and scourgeth every son whom be receiveth" (Heb. 12:6). Being chastened proves that we are children of God.

Lack of chastening proves that a person doesn't belong to the Lord. God says, "But if ye be without chastisement, whereof all [true children of God] are partakers, then are ye bastards, and not sons" (Heb. 12:8). Dr. Oliver B. Greene wrote concerning this subject, "The truth of this verse in plain language is that *any person who can practice sin, enjoy sin and prosper in it, has never been born of the Spirit and washed in the blood.* Spiritually, that person is illegitimate; he is a bastard. All born again, blood washed believers are chastened of the Lord."[221]

John Calvin wrote, "The profession of Christ would be false and deceitful if they withdrew themselves from the discipline of the Father, and they would become bastards. . . ."[222]

John Owen explained the issue this way: "Those who have only the name of Christians are called bastards or spurious or illegitimate children, because they are not born of God, being only children of the flesh—not Isaacs, but Ishmaels, whatever their profession."[223]

In his book *Hebrews Verse by Verse,* William R. Newell wrote, "A 'bastard' bears the family name—but does not *belong!* Of all dooms, to bear the *name* of a child of God, and not be a child, is worst!"[224]

Warren W. Wiersbe, in his exposition of Hebrews, made the following statements: "If I resisted God's will and did not experience His loving chastening, I would be afraid that I was not saved. All true children of God receive His chastening. All others who claim to be saved, but who escape chastening, are nothing but counterfeits—illegitimate children."[225]

Years ago in a church in Grand Rapids, Michigan, after I preached this truth, a young man approached me and asked to speak with me. We went into the pastor's study, and he told me that he claimed to be a Christian but was living in sin and that God was not chastening him. I thank God that he saw this truth, turned to God and trusted Christ as his personal Savior to become a real son of God, not a bastard.

Q

87. Why is there war around the world?

A

A short article in *U. S. News & World Report* stated, "A new study from a Washington think tank details a little known fact: Forty-five nations—a fourth of the world's countries—are now fighting wars."[226]

For thousands of years men have fought wars. In compiling an index of European wars, Professor Pitirim A. Sorokin of Harvard University and Nicholas N. Golovin, a former lieutenant general in the Imperial Russian army, learned that wars grew in number from 2,678 in the twelfth century to 13,835 in the first twenty-five years of the twentieth century.[227]

Dr. Harry Hager wrote:

In 3,358 years from 1496 B.C. to 1862 A.D. there were 227 years of peace and 3,130 years of war. Within the last three centuries there have been 286 major and minor wars in Europe. From the year 1500 B.C. to 1860 A.D. more than 8,000 treaties of peace, meant to remain in force forever, were negotiated. The average time they remained in force was two years.[228]

James told us why so many wars take place and where they originate: "From whence come wars and fightings among you? Come they not hence, even of your lusts that war in your members?" Wars and fightings come from the inside of men, and the origin is lust, the desire to get what one does not have and greatly desires. "Coveting what a man or nation does not have is the cause of war according to James."[229]

Albert Barnes traced the lustful desires that cause war: "Most of the wars which have occurred in the world can be traced to what the apostle here calls lusts. The desire of booty, the love of conquest, the ambition for extended rule, the gratification of revenge, these and similar causes have led to all the wars that have desolated the earth."[230]

A little boy came in from school one day and asked his mother, "Mama, how do wars get started?"

She replied, "Well, if you're talking about the last war, it got started when Germany attacked Belgium."

Dad, who had been buried in the evening newspaper, came up for air and said, "No, Son, it wasn't Belgium; it was when Germany attacked Poland."

But the mother insisted, "No, I'm sure I remember correctly; it was Belgium."

"Now what do you know about it?" corrected the father. "You didn't go to college. I did and I minored in world history. I tell you the war began when the Germans attacked Poland."

Before long the parents were arguing heatedly; soon they were shouting at each other. The little boy tugged at his mother, and she snapped at him, "Well, what do you want?"

He said, "That's OK, Mama. Now I think I know how wars get started."

Though wars and rumors of wars occur, thank God that Jesus Christ, the Prince of Peace, will soon return to this earth. Then the Scriptures will be fulfilled that say, "In his days shall the righteous flourish; and abundance of peace so long as the moon endureth"; "Of the increase of his government and peace there shall be no end"; "My people shall dwell in a peaceable habitation"; "And he shall speak peace unto the heathen" (Ps. 72:7; Isa. 9:7; 32:18; Zech. 9:10).

There will not and cannot be peace in this world until the Prince of Peace returns, yet the individual who will put his complete trust in Christ can have peace in his heart today. Christ's death on the cross made it possible that we—the enemies of God and the ones of whom Scripture said, "And the way of peace have they not known" (Rom. 3:17)—can have "peace with God" (Rom. 5:1) and "the peace of God" (Phil. 4:7). "Peace with God" comes when we trust Jesus Christ as our personal Savior and are justified by faith in Him. Paul tells us how we can know the peace of God: "Be careful for nothing; but in every thing by prayer and supplication with thanksgiving let your requests be made known unto God. And the peace of God, which passeth all understanding, shall keep your hearts and minds through Christ Jesus" (Phil. 4:6, 7). He says that we are to be anxious for nothing, but prayerful about everything.

My prayer for the reader is this: "The LORD bless thee, and keep thee: The LORD make his face shine upon thee, and be gracious unto thee: The LORD lift up his countenance upon thee, and give thee peace" (Num. 6:24–26).

Q

88. How many angels are there?

A

Thirty-four books of the Bible mention angels. They appear 108 times in the Old Testament and 165 times in the New Testament.

God created angels sometime before He created the world (Job 38:1, 4, 7). Although they were created without fault, one third of them followed Satan in his rebellion against God (Rev. 12:3, 4). Since their rebellion, the Bible refers to the ones who followed Satan as the Devil's angels (Matt. 25:41; Rev. 12:9) and to those who did not rebel as holy and elect angels (Mark 8:38; 1 Tim. 5:21).

The holy angels are "ministering spirits, sent forth to minister for them who shall be heirs of salvation" (Heb. 1:13, 14). They will spend eternity in the Holy City, New Jerusalem (Heb. 12:22, 23). The evil angels are those angels who "kept not their first estate, but left their own habitation," and they are "reserved in everlasting chains under darkness unto the judgment of the great day" (Jude 6). They will finally be consigned to everlasting fire, which is "prepared for the devil and his angels" (Matt. 25:41).

The Bible says their number is large. Concerning angels Daniel wrote, "Thousand thousands ministered unto him, and ten thousand times ten thousand stood before him" (Dan. 7:10). John said, "And I beheld, and I heard the voice of many angels round about the throne and the beasts and the elders: and the number of them was ten thousand times ten thousand, and thousands of thousands" (Rev. 5:11). Hebrews 12:22 refers to "an innumerable company of angels." Ten thousand times ten thousand is 100 million, plus thousands of thousands. Only God knows their total number.

Dr. A. C. Gaebelein wrote about the practical value of this truth concerning angels:

> *Like every truth, the truth of the angels of God, their presence on earth and their loving ministries, has practical value. As we realize in faith that we are the objects of observation of so many unseen beings, the host of angels, and, think of it, that they are watching us, ready to walk with us, as we walk with Him in His ways, ready to serve us as we serve Him, ready to shield us and help us in a hundred different ways, a solemn feeling will come into our lives.*

Surely we shall walk softly in the presence of the Lord and His holy angels. We shall remember that they also are witnesses of our deeds and listen to our words. Thus this truth will assist us in a holy life. Furthermore, as we remember that they are about us for our preservation and protection we can live for Him and serve Him without fearing the power of the enemy, knowing that our Lord will keep us in all His ways.[231]

Q 89. Will there be two resurrections, and, if so, who will be raised at each one?

A Many Christians believe that only one general resurrection will take place, in which all the dead will be raised. But some other people do not believe any resurrection will occur. The Bible records this question: "If a man die, shall he live again?" (Job 14:14). Jesus answered that question in John 5:28 and 29: "Marvel not at this: for the hour is coming, in the which all that are in the graves shall hear his voice, and shall come forth; they that have done good, unto the resurrection of life; and they that have done evil, unto the resurrection of damnation." Notice the two resurrections: "the resurrection of life" and "the resurrection of damnation." Paul spoke of the two resurrections: "There shall be a resurrection of the dead, both of the just and unjust" (Acts 24:15). He also asked the question: "Why should it be thought a thing incredible with you, that God should raise the dead?" (Acts 26:8).

In referring to the resurrection Paul wrote, "but every man in his own order . . ." (1 Cor. 15:23). According to Greek scholars, the word "order" *(tagma)* is a military term denoting a company, troop, band, division or rank. The dead will be raised in three main ranks or divisions.

Using the analogy of harvest, the Bible describes Christ as "the firstfruits" (1 Cor. 15:23). He is the firstfruits (leader) of the harvest (resurrection). His example promises an abundance of similar fruits that will follow at the time of harvest. His resurrection marks the beginning of the program of resurrection.

A number of people were raised from the dead during Old Testament times, but they later died a second time. Christ raised some people from the dead during His ministry, and a few were raised during the period of the apostles, but all of them died again. Christ is the first One to rise from the dead and be no longer subject to death.

The second division to be raised are "they [who] are Christ's at his coming" (1 Cor. 15:23). All believers of all ages fit into this rank.

This group includes those who will be resurrected when Christ comes for His own at the Rapture. "For the Lord himself shall descend from heaven with a shout, with the voice of the archangel, and with the trump of God: and the dead in Christ shall rise first" (1 Thess. 4:16). When Christ comes for His own, He will bring with Him the souls and spirits of those who sleep in Jesus. The bodies of the dead in Christ will be reunited with their souls and spirits in resurrection, and they will then meet the Lord in the air (1 Thess 4:14–17).

This group also includes the saved Jews and Gentiles of the Old Testament (Dan. 12:1, 2; Isa. 26:19–21) together with the martyrs of the tribulation period (Rev. 20:4). The martyrs will be raised from the dead and will reign with Christ for a thousand years.

"But the rest of the dead lived not again until the thousand years were finished. This is the first resurrection" (Rev. 20:5). The first resurrection includes all who will have risen from the dead before the Millennium—Christ, the Church saints, the Old Testament saints and the martyred saints of the tribulation period.

First Corinthians 15:24 says, "Then cometh the end. . . ." The third rank of those to be resurrected are the wicked dead. Their resurrection will take place at the end of the thousand-year reign of Christ on the earth. They will be judged according to their works and then will be cast into the Lake of Fire (Rev. 20:5; 20:11–15).

J. Dwight Pentecost wrote concerning the resurrections:

The order of events in the resurrection program would be: (1) the resurrection of Christ as the beginning of the resurrection program (I Cor. 15:23); (2) the resurrection of the Church age saints at the rapture (I Thess. 4:16); (3) the resurrection of the tribulation period saints (Rev. 20:3–5), together with (4) the resurrection of Old Testament saints (Dan. 12:2; Isa. 26:19) at the second advent of Christ to the earth; and finally (5) the final resurrection of the unsaved dead (Rev. 20:11–14) at the end of the millennial age. The first four stages would all be included in the first resurrection or resurrection to life, inasmuch as all receive eternal life and the last would be the second resurrection, or the resurrection unto damnation, inasmuch as all receive eternal judgment at that time.[232]

God's Word promises, "Blessed and holy is he that hath part in the first resurrection: on such the second death hath no power, but they shall be priests of God and of Christ, and shall reign with him a thousand years" (Rev. 20:6). The saved will be happy and holy and will have part in the first resurrection. The second death will have no power over them. This fact means they will never go to the Lake of Fire (which is the second death [Rev. 20:14]). They will be priests of God and of Christ and will reign with Him a thousand years.

What a difference for the unsaved! Instead of having a part in the first resurrection, they will "have their part in the lake which burneth with fire and brimstone: which is the second death" (Rev. 21:8). Which part will you have?

Q 90. Where do you get your percentage that only 2 percent of people living today are saved?

A I first saw this percentage in the book *Profiles of Prophecy* by Dr. S. Franklin Logsdon, who at one time was pastor of the Moody Memorial Church in Chicago. He wrote in his book:

> *Those who are worrying about the so-called population explosion in the world would do well to leave these matters with the Lord. He not only has all things under control, but actually has revealed what will transpire in this connection. Peruse the following statistics:*
>
> *25% die during the 4th seal judgment (Rev. 6:8)*
>
> *33% die during the 6th trumpet judgment (Rev. 9:18). This leaves just 50% of the earth's population.*
>
> *2% will have gone when the Church was raptured (2% said to be total of those vitally Christian)*
>
> *Subtract martyrs killed during the 5th Seal Judgment (Rev. 6:9)*
>
> *Subtract the "many" who die during the 3rd trumpet judgment (Rev. 8:11)*
>
> *RESULT: Less than one-half of the earth's population will be left.*[233]

The second time I saw this percentage was when I read the book *Evangelism* by James A. Stewart, who was mightily used of God in evangelism and revival in Europe and America. Many times he spoke to thousands daily. He wrote:

> It is a cold and sobering fact that not two percent of the world's population are evangelical believers. *More than half of our brothers and sisters, bound with us in the natural ties of humanity, have never once heard the Gospel of our peerless Redeemer. . . . Even in our outstanding evangelistic campaigns in America and the British Empire, usually only five percent of the fruit remains.*[234]

Leonard Ravenhill wrote, "One of the top ten evangelists mourns that only half of one percent of his converts endure. Another declares that a year after their decision, not ten percent of converts show any sign of regeneration."[235]

I have read articles by missionaries who say that at least 2.7 billion people living in the world today have never heard one clear presentation of the gospel. That is more than half the world's population. Then hundreds of millions of unsaved people belong to false religions and cults. George Gallup, Jr., says that 70 percent of Americans are members of churches.[236]

Men of God of the past and present believe that at least 90 percent of church members in America are lost.

David Barrett, statistician for religion and editor of *The Christian World Encyclopedia* in Richmond, Virginia, published a prognosis for the year 2000: Of the 6.25 billion people on earth, there will be 1.2 billion Moslems, 860 million Hindus, 360 million Buddhists and 260 million atheists. One billion will be indifferent. Counting the unevangelized, those in false religions and cults, the atheists and the indifferent, it's not difficult to believe that only about 2 percent of the people of the world are saved.

Those who are saved have a responsibility to take the gospel to those who aren't. Jesus commanded, "Go ye into all the world, and preach the gospel to every creature" (Mark 16:15).

Q 91. Will the Lord hold accountable the millions of people who never heard the gospel message?

A A person's answer to this question determines to a large extent his interest in foreign missions, his giving to missions and his going to the mission field. This question is important, and we must not base our answer on human reasoning but on the Word of God.

God's Word makes it plain that everyone is lost without Christ. For example, Romans 2:12 states, "For as many as have sinned without law shall also perish without law: and as many as have sinned in the law shall be judged by the law." Another example is Romans 3:12, which declares, "They are all gone out of the way, they are together become unprofitable; there is none that doeth good, no, not one." And the well-known verse Romans 3:23 sends the same message: "For all have sinned, and come short of the glory of God." We could quote many other references, such as Romans 3:9–19, 2 Corinthians 4:3 and 4, Ephesians 2:1–3 and Revelation 21:8, to name a few.

God's Word makes it plain that people are saved only through Christ. John 3:18 says, "He that believeth on him [Christ] is not condemned: but he that believeth not is condemned already, because he hath not believed in the name of the only begotten Son of God." John 3:36 gives the same message in different words: "He that believeth on the Son hath everlasting life: and he that believeth not the Son shall not see life; but the wrath of God abideth on him." Christ Himself declared, "I am the way, the truth, and the life: no man cometh unto the Father, but by me" (John 14:6). The apostles proclaimed the same message. Peter told the Jewish leaders, "Neither is there salvation in any other: for there is none other name under heaven given among men, whereby we must be saved" (Acts 4:12). Paul wrote to Timothy, "For there is one God, and one mediator between God and men, the man Christ Jesus" (1 Tim. 2:5). And John declared, "He that hath the Son hath life; and he that hath not the Son of God hath not life" (1 John 5:12).

God gives every person some light (spiritual illumination; something that enlightens and informs): the light of creation and the light of conscience.

Concerning the light of creation, the Bible says, "For the invisible things of him from the creation of the world are clearly seen, being understood by the things that are made, even his eternal power and Godhead; so that they are without excuse" (Rom. 1:20). "The heavens declare the glory of God; and the firmament sheweth his handywork" (Ps. 19:1). "He hath set eternity in their heart" (Eccles. 3:11, ASV).

God has revealed Himself to man in creation, but man has turned from that light and rejected it, worshiping the creature rather than the Creator: "Who changed the truth of God into a lie, and worshipped and served the creature more than the Creator" (Rom. 1:25).

Man also has the light of conscience: "For when the Gentiles, which have not the law, do by nature the things contained in the law, these, having not the law, are a law unto themselves: which shew the work of the law written in their hearts, their conscience also bearing witness, and their thoughts the mean while accusing or else excusing one another" (Rom. 2:14, 15).

G. Christian Weiss, past director of the Missions Department of the Back to the Bible Broadcast, explained:

The heathen are condemned, not for rejecting Christ, but for sinning against light which they already have and doing it deliberately. The heathen themselves admit that they are not living up to the light they have and often readily confess that they know themselves to be lost. Even when they had the gospel, many of them deliberately reject it.[237]

At the Great White Throne Judgment, Christ will judge the unsaved according to their works: "And the dead were judged out of those things which were written in the books, according to their works" (Rev. 20:12).

Mr. Weiss continued on this subject:

The heathen will not be punished unjustly. They will not be punished for rejecting a Savior whom they have never heard about but they will be judged and separated from God because they deliberately rejected Him, as God and the light He gave them, and they will be punished according to the degree of that light which they possessed and the sins which they deliberately committed.[238]

God will provide the way of salvation to those who really want to be saved. God is "a rewarder of them that diligently seek him" (Heb. 11:6). God sent Peter to the home of Cornelius, a Roman official, who

156

wanted to be saved but didn't know the way of salvation. God told Cornelius, "Send men to Joppa, and call for Simon, whose surname is Peter; who shall tell thee words, whereby thou and all thy house shall be saved" (Acts 11:13, 14). When Peter preached Christ to Cornelius, his kinsmen and near friends, they believed on the Lord Jesus Christ and were saved (Acts 10).

Christians are responsible to get the gospel to those who have not heard it. Christ gave to the Church the Great Commission, which is recorded five times in the New Testament: Matthew 28:19 and 20; Mark 16:15; Luke 24:47 and 48; John 20:21; Acts 1:8. We are commanded, "Go ye into all the world, and preach the gospel to every creature" (Mark 16:15).

May God stir our hearts to pray, give and go so that the unsaved may hear and be saved. If you are not a Christian, receive the Lord Jesus Christ as your personal Savior. Someone has said, "If you are worried about the people outside [of Christianity], the most unreasonable thing you can do is to remain outside yourself."

Q 92. Is there an unpardonable sin, and, if so, what is it?

A It will surprise many people to learn that the Bible makes no mention of an "unpardonable" sin. Three passages in the New Testament tell us that blasphemy against the Holy Spirit could occur and that those who committed that sin "shall not be forgiven," "hath never forgiveness," "shall not be forgiven" (Matt. 12:31, 32; Mark 3:28–30; Luke 12:10).

The fear of having committed this sin troubles a great many people. The blasphemy against the Holy Spirit consists in saying that the works of Christ, which were done by the Holy Spirit, were done by the Devil (Matt. 12:22–32). A number of Bible scholars see no possibility of this sin's being committed today. Dr. Lewis Sperry Chafer concluded, "It is therefore impossible for this particular sin to be committed today. . . . The possibility of this particular sin being committed ceased with Christ's removal from the earth."[239]

Dr. Homer A. Kent, Jr., wrote concerning this subject, "The real possibility of this sin does not weaken the gospel invitation 'Whosoever will,' for by its very nature such will have no willingness to accept.

As for the Pharisees of Jesus' audience, it is not stated whether or not they had fully committed this sin, but the warning is clear."[240]

Another question arises: "If you are a Christian and commit the unpardonable sin, what happens?" A Christian can never commit this sin—Christ pardoned and forgave all his sins. God promised those who are saved that "your sins are forgiven you for his name's sake" (1 John 2:12).

Q 93. What is the "sin unto death"?

A First John 5:16 refers to the sin unto death: "If any man see his brother sin a sin which is not unto death, he shall ask, and he shall give him life for them that sin not unto death. There is a sin unto death: I do not say that he shall pray for it." Many people are confused about this sin. Some confuse it with the unpardonable sin. Others think that a Christian will lose his salvation if he commits this sin.

Only Christians can commit the sin unto death. The verse above definitely refers to a Christian because of the term "his brother." The sin is not a specific sin, but sin persisted in by a believer. The indefinite article "a" does not appear; it could be rendered, not "a sin unto death," but "sin unto death." Dr. Harry Ironside stated that "it is not that there is some specific sin that always results in death, but there is sin unto death."[241]

This verse (1 John 5:16) refers to physical death, because no true Christian can die spiritually (John 11:25, 26). When a child of God continues in sin and does not confess and forsake his sin after God has chastised him, God sometimes takes his life. The writer of Hebrews wrote concerning this subject:

> For whom the Lord loveth he chasteneth, and scourgeth every son whom he receiveth. If ye endure chastening, God dealeth with you as with sons; for what son is he whom the father chasteneth not? But if ye be without chastisement, whereof all are partakers, then are ye bastards, and not sons. Furthermore we have had fathers of our flesh which corrected us, and we gave them reverence: shall we not much rather be in subjection unto the Father of spirits, and live?" (Heb. 12:6–9).

Notice the last two words "and live." I think we could conclude that if we do not respond to God's chastening, we will not live, but will die physically.

Proverbs 15:10 claims that "correction is grievous unto him that forsaketh the way: and he that hateth reproof shall die." God does try to correct His children when they sin. But this correction oppresses and distresses some of them, and they come to hate reproof. A person can be grieved at God's correction until he comes to hate God's reproof, and then it is the sin unto death.

Moses committed sin unto death when he lost his temper and struck the rock instead of speaking to it as he had been commanded to do (Num. 20:7–12; Deut. 32:48–52; 34:5–7). Ananias and Sapphira committed sin unto death when they lied to God (Acts 5:1–11).

The Corinthian Christians committed sin unto death by their carelessness and disorderly conduct at the observance of the Lord's Supper. They experienced the chastening of God so that many of them were weak and sickly, and many slept (died) (1 Cor. 11:30). If they had judged themselves, God would not have had to judge them (1 Cor. 11:31).

Dr. Harry Ironside told the story of a young man who committed sin unto death:

> I once knew a splendid young man who left his home in obedience to what he believed to be the call of God to engage in Christian work in a needy district. He had not been there long before a proposition for a very good temporal position came between him and the Lord. Then too the young woman who he desired to marry declared that she would never marry a preacher, and so he decided to take the position. He settled down, made money, and got ahead, but inwardly was always very unhappy. He knew that he had sinned against the Lord because he had been called to a different service. By and by tuberculosis laid hold of him. He gave up his position and spent the earnings of years in a sanitorium, where he lay flat on his back. I was near by, and he sent for me and said, "My brother, I want you to pray with me, but not that the Lord will raise me up, unless He should make it very clear to you that it is His will. I have been facing a great many things here lately. I see my failure now as never before. I believe I have sinned unto death." I looked to the Lord asking, if it was His will, to lift him up, but if not, to give him great joy in departing. Two weeks later I saw him again and

he said, "I will never see you on earth again. I have had two very wonderful weeks. The Lord has been very near to me, but He has told me that He is going to take me home, that I lost my opportunity, and that inasmuch as I chose my own comfort instead of His will He can't trust me here any more. But, thank God, I am perfectly resigned to His will. I am going home!" And, sure enough, three days later he died. He had sinned unto death, and it was useless to pray for his healing, but he went home happy in Christ.[242]

It's very important that we as Christians deal with our sins honestly and confess them immediately. A good rule is "Keep short accounts with God." Regarding lightly the chastening of the Lord could result in sin unto death. Let us take His chastening seriously and submissively.

I heard Dr. Fred Brown say in one of his messages, "If a Christian is true and faithful to the Lord, He will take that Christian home and crown him. If a Christian is not true and faithful, the Lord will crown him and take him home."

Q 94. Will the world be here sometime in the next century?

A If you were to ask some educators, scientists and statesmen this question, they would answer, "No." Hear their words:

Andrei Sakharov, Russian scientist—"The pulling of a few levers, the pushing of a few buttons, and the throwing of a few switches would result in the complete annihilation of every living thing on earth."[243]

Alan Munn, physicist—"Man could be obliterated from this world in two to three minutes."[244]

Frank Sterrett, veteran writer and photographer—

Here is my guess. The year 2000 will be the last year of man to exist on this planet. What is the cause of my thinking? My answer is, the population explosion first and foremost. Next, pollution, air, water, and soil. From my observations, the world is going to hell, downhill with the brakes off, and it doesn't seem that man is trying or can do anything about it.[245]

Walter Spears—

I had a letter of introduction to the Professor of Political Economy in Cambridge, who is also one of the editors of the Manchester Guardian. *I met him one day on deck and remarked upon how terrible he looked, and asked him if he was sick. He said he was not, but that he had been up all night with a group of men in someone's cabin discussing world affairs. The group of men turned out to be the head of another government, an air chief marshall, a famous war correspondent and author, a radio news analyst, an attorney general, and himself. He said they had been discussing the whole night long the conditions in the world and looking for some pinpoint of hope, and they found none. Finally about 4:00 A.M. one of the men present summed up the discussion by saying, "There is every evidence to indicate that this is the end of the world, and that mankind is the composite devil who is going to destroy himself."*[246]

During a TV discussion on a British forum the subject was this: "What sort of a world will we have by the year 2000?" With only a single exception, every scientist on the forum said in substance, "The world won't be here."

Even young people are running scared. A thirteen-year-old Iowa girl polled 370 junior high school students, and 75 percent of them said they are afraid they will die in a nuclear war during the next ten years.

The Word of God makes it clear that the world will be here in the next century and not only in the next century but also for at least 1,007 years. If Christ were to come today (and He may), the seven-year tribulation period would take place, after which Jesus would come to this earth and rule for 1,000 years. Then, and only then, will the earth be burned up (2 Pet. 3:10–13). Therefore, this planet will be here for a long time. At the close of the Millennium God will destroy it by fire, but He promised that we can, "according to his promise, look for new heavens and a new earth, wherein dwelleth righteousness" (2 Pet. 3:13).

Q 95. Will the Church continue to weaken until the day the Lord comes?

A Yes, I believe the church will continue to weaken. I read a tract written by an unknown writer and published by the Lutheran Colportage Service of Minneapolis, Minnesota. It describes the times we are living in accurately. It is titled "Just Before Jesus Comes."

Paul wrote to the Thessalonians that before the coming of our Lord there should come a falling away first, II Thess. 2:3, and to Timothy he stated that evil men and imposters should wax worse and worse, and that there should be perilous times in the last days, II Tim. 3:1–13. It will be noticed in the Scriptures that the apostasy is not concerning education, or fine churches, or able ministers, or large congregations, or the progress of intellectual and material prosperity, but the breaking down that is foretold of the visible church is on faith, and a denial of the power of God in Holy Ghost experience. There is present well-nigh a universal landslide in the visible church towards higher criticism, which is lower infidelism, and a denial of the supernatural working of God in regeneration, definite answers to prayer, and the revelation of divine things to the soul by the Holy Spirit, which make up the religion of the Apostles and their true successors.

We are then to expect great deceptions and delusions, deceiving, if it were possible, the very elect.

We may also expect great advances in the "form of godliness" in the last days. Faith will not become low through worldliness and the denial of the Scriptures only, but through the remarkable imitative faiths which will work on in their deceptive power. A pastor says,

"These movements will become an unseen influence in the air around us; an atmosphere peopled with evil spirits, and heavy with the depression of hell. These evil spirits will do their utmost to injure, mislead, confuse, and depress the children of the Lord. Our bodies will be affected; it will prey on our minds and becloud our

souls. All kinds of strange feelings and new and peculiar trials will come to us. A surprising lack of desire and energy, Godward, a spiritual deadness, a mental heaviness, lethargy of soul, an alarming desire for forbidden things and a peculiar delight and fascination in any of the world's pleasures we dare taste. It will be difficult to preach the Word in liberty and power; it will be difficult to give attention to the Word when it is preached; it will be very difficult to get down to real earnest and continued prayer. This is the atmosphere in which we must battle as the days darken around us. Oh, let us be strong in the Lord! Satan will no doubt bring a mysterious power to bear on our minds and wills, which will make it exceedingly difficult to walk closely with God, and very easy to live in the flesh. We will be amazed at the power he can use against us. It will become very hard to serve God faithfully, and to pray earnestly. It will seem as if everything without us, and almost everything within us, has conspired to keep us from following Christ all the way, and to induce us to compromise; we will be surrounded by a worldly atmosphere that will draw us away from God, that will render prayer half-hearted, and that will deaden our spiritual senses to the reality of Heavenly things, and the glorious presence of the Lord. It will become very easy to slip out of communion with God, and harder than ever to keep the communication open between our souls and Heaven."

Already we feel the beginning of the influence of the inrush of these things upon us. Worldliness in various forms weaves its ever-expanding power over many congregations. Things are not only allowed, but are unblushingly organized now, which would not have been possible a generation since. The craze for the Drama and the exciting round of pleasure is catered to in connection with many places of worship, to the destroying of deep spirituality, the bringing to an end of revivals and the furtherance of the spirit of compromise with doubtful things and associations.

There is a terrible decline of faith and true religion all over the world at this moment. We do not deny that there may be here and there exceptions, but looking at Christendom as a whole it presents a sad picture.

Reviewing these matters, do they not constitute a loud call to the servants of Christ to arise, and seek during the intervening short

*period, to make the most of this the day of opportunity, before
their Lord and Master comes to summon them to give an account
of their labors at the Judgement Seat of Christ?*

Peter wrote about the Day of the Lord, when "the elements shall
melt with fervent heat, the earth also and the works that are therein
shall be burned up" (2 Pet. 3:10). Then he asked the question, "What
manner of persons ought ye to be?" (v. 11). He answered the question
as he continued to write the rest of chapter 3. In light of the fact that
apostasy is widespread and that Jesus may come at any moment, he
told us ten things we ought to be in times like these:

1. We ought to be holy people. In verse 11 Peter used the phrase
   "holy conversation," which means a holy manner of life. This
   term basically means set apart for the service of God.
2. We ought to be godly people. In verse 11 Peter also referred
   to godliness, which means something "characterized by a
   Godward attitude," something that "does that which is well-
   pleasing to him."
3. We ought to be people who look for His coming. Verse 12
   exhorts us to be "looking for," which means "to expect or wait
   for." Paul said in Philippians 3:20, "For our conversation
   [citizenship] is in heaven: from whence also we look for the
   Saviour, the Lord Jesus Christ."
4. We ought to be people who earnestly desire His coming.
   "Hasting" means "earnestly desiring." Paul wrote that we
   should "love his appearing" (2 Tim. 4:8).
5. We ought to be diligent people. Peter exhorted us to be
   "diligent," which means "do your best, make haste, take care,
   hurry on." Jesus encouraged His servants, "Occupy till I
   come" (Luke 19:13), which means "to buy up the opportunities, to be busy."
6. We ought to be peaceful people. Peter told us to "be diligent
   that ye may be found of him in peace." Dr. Kenneth S.
   Wuest commented that the phrase "in peace" refers to peace
   among the saints. Christians should make every effort to live
   peacefully with others.
7. We ought to be spotless people. In verse 14 Peter said we
   should be "without spot," which means "being free from
   censure, irreproachable, free from all defilement in the sight
   of God."

8. We ought to be blameless people. "Blameless" speaks of what cannot be blamed or found fault with. Paul prayed for Christians, "I pray God your whole spirit and soul and body be preserved blameless unto the coming of our Lord Jesus Christ" (1 Thess. 5:23).

9. We ought to be people who are on guard. Peter wrote, "Ye therefore, beloved, seeing ye know these things before, beware lest ye also, being led away with the error of the wicked, fall from your own stedfastness" (2 Pet. 3:17). "Beware" is a military term meaning "to guard or be on your guard." We need to be on guard lest we be drawn away from the faith by the error of the wicked and, as a consequence, lose our own steadfastness.

10. We ought to be growing people. This is the last of Peter's exhortations to us in chapter 3 of his second epistle. We are to grow in grace, which means growing in the Christian life, growing in our love for the Lord Jesus Christ and growing up "into him in all things, which is the head, even Christ" (Eph. 4:15).

We are also to grow in the knowledge of our Lord and Savior Jesus Christ, which means really getting to know and understand Him completely. Paul prayed, "That I might know him, and the power of his resurrection, and the fellowship of his sufferings, being made conformable unto his death" (Phil. 3:10).

I believe Christians can arrest the trend of weakness in our churches by being holy and godly; by looking for His coming; by earnestly desiring His coming; by being diligent, peaceful, without spot, blameless, and on guard; and by growing. Jesus said of Christians, "Ye are the salt of the earth" (Matt. 5:13). One of the purposes of salt is to preserve from corruption. May God help each of us to be a "salty" Christian and help preserve this decaying world.

Q 96. How can I know that I am saved?

A For the first twenty-six years of my life I was an agnostic. The word "agnostic" comes from two Greek words—*a,* meaning "without"; and *gnosko,* meaning "I know."

Agnosko means "without knowledge" or "I know not."

When I was twenty-six, God saved me. He has given me the blessed assurance that I have eternal life. I thank God that I *know* I am saved.

First John 5:13 gives us this precious promise: "These things have I written unto you that believe on the name of the Son of God; that ye may know that ye have eternal life, and that ye may believe on the name of the Son of God." The book of 1 John has only 5 chapters and 105 verses. Nevertheless, that short book uses the word "know" twenty-seven times, "knoweth" six times, "known" five times and "knew" one time—for a total of thirty-nine times. God wants us to *know* we are saved.

Let me give three reasons I know I am saved and how you can know you are saved.

1. His work *for* me makes me sure. My salvation and yours depends entirely upon what the Lord Jesus Christ has done for us. He fulfilled all the requirements of the broken law, the law that we had broken. Our sins were laid upon Him, and He paid the full penalty in our place. "But he was wounded for our transgressions, he was bruised for our iniquities: the chastisement of our peace was upon him; and with his stripes we are healed. All we like sheep have gone astray; we have turned every one to his own way; and the LORD hath laid on him the iniquity of us all" (Isa. 53:5, 6). Those of us who have received the Lord Jesus Christ as our personal Savior have already passed from death to life. The words of Jesus Himself assure us of this truth: "Verily, verily, I say unto you, He that heareth my word, and believeth on him that sent me, hath everlasting life, and shall not come unto condemnation; but is passed from death unto life" (John 5:24). Three truths stand out in this verse: the person who truly believes on the Lord Jesus Christ "hath everlasting life," "shall not come into condemnation" and "is passed from death unto life."

> *Upon a life I did not live,*
> *Upon a death I did not die,*
> *Another's life, another's death,*
> *I stake my whole eternity.*[247]

2. His Word *to* me makes me sure. The blood of Christ makes me safe; the Word of God makes me sure. God's Word clearly states, "But as many as received him [Christ], to them gave he power to become the

sons of God, even to them that believe on his name" (John 1:12). I have received Him and believed on Him, and He has given me power (authority or right) to become His son. He promised in John 3:16 that those who believe on Him should not perish but have everlasting life. I believed on the Lord Jesus Christ, and He gave me everlasting life, which means I will never perish. Acts 13:38 and 39 tell us "all that believe are justified from all things." To be justified means we are declared righteous. Scofield said concerning justification, "The justified believer has been in court, only to learn that nothing is laid to his charge."[248]

God says in Acts 16:31, "Believe on the Lord Jesus Christ, and thou shalt be saved." I have believed on Him, and I am saved.

In Romans 10:9 God promised, "That if thou shalt confess with thy mouth the Lord Jesus, and shalt believe in thine heart that God hath raised him from the dead, thou shalt be saved." I have confessed Christ with my mouth and believed in my heart that God has raised Him from the dead. God says, therefore, that I am saved.

First John 5:12 says, "He that hath the Son hath life." I have the Son because I received Him. God declares that I have (eternal) life.

I could quote scores of verses that assure me—and all those who truly believe on the Lord Jesus Christ as their personal Savior—that I am (we are) saved.

A preacher related this incident that occurred while he preached in the south of Ireland:

After my message, as I spoke to the people, I asked an elderly lady, "I trust you now know the salvation of God, and have eternal life."

"I hope so," she replied, showing no desire to pass me.

"But why should you only 'hope,' my friend, when God wishes you to 'know' that if you believe in His Son, you have eternal life?"

"Well, sir, I believe in the Son of God. And all I can say is I 'hope,' and I don't think anyone can 'know' as long as they are in this world."

"If you will permit me," I answered, "I will show you just one little verse in the Word of God that will settle the matter definitely."

"You need not trouble yourself," she declared. "I know the Word of God well. Ever since I was a child I have studied it, and I don't

believe there is a verse you can show me that I don't know."

"Just one?"

"Well, where is it?" she asked.

Taking her large print Bible from her hands, I found and read to her, "These things have I written unto you that believe on the name of the Son of God; that ye may know that ye have eternal life" (1 John 5:13). I read it a second time and then said, "Do you believe on the name of the Son of God?"

"I do," came her emphatic reply.

"You really do own that you are a lost sinner needing salvation and that nothing but the blood-shedding of the Son of God could avail to put away your sins?"

"I do."

"You repudiate all thought of salvation by your own works, confess that you are an undone and guilty lost sinner, and now you simply believe in the name of the Son of God?"

"I do," came again the short and sincere answer.

"Well, then, granting all that, have you eternal life?"

"I hope so."

"Oh," was my reply. "I see it now. In the days when you went to school, which was, of course, a great while ago, they used to spell differently than from now."

"How so, sir?"

"Why, K-N-O-W used to spell hope in those days."

"Not at all, sir."

"What did they spell?"

"Why, of course, they spelled know, the same then as now."

"There is a mistake somewhere," I replied. "There must be, for you say you believe on the name of the Son of God. And He says, 'These things have I written unto you that believe on the name of the Son of God; that ye may know that ye have eternal life,' and you stand

there and tell me that you only hope you have it."

"Let me see that verse myself," said the old lady.

The Spirit of God blessed her perusal of the sacred message and filled her heart with peace as she believed it. "Hope" died on the spot, and faith and amazement mingled had taken possession of her soul.

3. His witness *in* me makes me sure. This witness is twofold. First is the witness of the Holy Spirit. The moment God saves us, the Holy Spirit enters our bodies to abide with us forever (John 14:16), and "The Spirit itself beareth witness with our spirit, that we are the children of God" (Rom. 8:16). "And because ye are sons, God hath sent forth the Spirit of his Son into your hearts, crying, Abba, Father" (Gal. 4:6). "He that believeth on the Son of God hath the witness in himself" (1 John 5:10). The Holy Spirit living in the Christian gives inward assurance of salvation.

> The Spirit answers to the blood,
> And tells me I am born of God.[249]

Second is the witness of a changed life. "Therefore if any man be in Christ, he is a new creature: old things are passed away; behold, all things are become new" (2 Cor. 5:17). These words become gloriously true when we are saved. "The things I once loved I now hate, and the things I once hated I now love." I love the things of God: His Word, His fellowship, His house, His people, His service. I hate the things of sin in which I once lived. I thoroughly enjoy life and am not afraid of death. "One thing I know, that, whereas I was blind, now I see" (John 9:25).

Q 97. How can I keep from worrying about the future?

A Charles F. Kettering said, "My interest is in the future because I am going to spend the rest of my life there."[250] I, too, am interested in the future, not only the future in this life but also in eternity.

Everyone is interested in the future. Young people are interested in knowing the future and in finding their place in it because the future is vague, uncertain and unknown. Dr. Kenneth O. Gangel was asked to speak to a crowd of 1,500 teens. He related that in responding to the invitation, he asked the director of the organization what topics he thought would interest and help the young people. Without a moment's hesitation the director responded, "Speak on prophecy."[251] Teens want to know what God has planned for the future.

When I give children and teenagers the opportunity to ask questions in my summer camp ministry, most of them ask questions concerning the future—questions about Heaven, Hell, the second coming of Christ, and so forth.

Jesus spoke of "men's hearts failing them for fear, and for looking after those things which are coming on the earth" (Luke 21:26). He also gave us a prescription for heart trouble. "Peace I leave with you, my peace I give unto you: not as the world giveth, give I unto you. Let not your heart be troubled, neither let it be afraid" (John 14:27). In the fourteenth chapter of John, Jesus told us how we can be unafraid and how to keep from worrying:

- Believe in God and Christ (v. 1).
- Believe there are many mansions for His children (v. 2).
- Realize Christ is coming back to receive His own (v. 3).
- Know that His children will be where He is (v. 3).
- Believe that Christ is the only way to Heaven (v. 6).
- Do the works He wants us to do (v. 12).
- Know that He answers prayer (vv. 13, 14).
- Realize His Holy Spirit is with His people forever (vv. 16–18).
- Rejoice in the truth that we shall live forever (v. 19).
- Accept the peace of God that He gives (v. 27).

Dr. Francis W. Dixon, English writer and speaker, wrote how to be cured of heart trouble:

> *You must trust in God as your loving Heavenly Father, rely on Jesus Christ as your own personal Saviour, believe in Heaven as your eternal Home, rejoice that Jesus is coming again, make full use of the privilege of prayer, recognize the Holy Spirit as your indwelling Comforter and receive Christ's peace to fill your heart—and as you do this you will be cured from heart trouble!*[252]

If I were unsaved and didn't know I am going to be with God and His people forever, I would be a frightened man. As I think of the terrible judgments ahead, when about three billion people will die in a short seven-year tribulation period, I thank God for saving me and keeping me from worrying about the future. I sing with the song writers,

> *I don't worry o'er the future,*
> *For I know what Jesus said,*
> *And Today I'll walk beside Him,*
> *For He knows what is ahead.*
>
> *Many things about tomorrow*
> *I don't seem to understand;*
> *But I know Who holds tomorrow,*
> *And I know Who holds my hand.*
> *—Ira Stanphill*

Stuart Hamblen wrote in one of his songs, "I know not what the future holds, but I know Who holds the future."

Someone else has said,

> *You can't change the past,*
> *But you can ruin a perfectly good present*
> *By worrying about the future.*

End Notes

1. M. R. DeHaan, *Coming Events in Prophecy* (Grand Rapids: Zondervan Publishing House, 1962), p. 9.

2. Jeffery L. Sheler, "A Revelation in the Middle East," *U.S. News & World Report,* November 19, 1990, pp. 67, 68.

3. E. Schuyler English, ed., Pilgrim Bible (New York: Oxford University Press, Inc., 1948), p. 926.

4. John Phillips, *Exploring Revelation* (Chicago: Moody Press, 1987), pp. 168, 169.

5. William L. Pettingill, "Evangelism: Specific Problems," *Bible Questions Answered* (Grand Rapids: Zondervan Publishing House, 1979), p. 135.

6. W. Myrddin Lewis, *Hidden Mysteries* (Glasgow: By the Author, 1965), p. 107.

7. Keith L. Brooks, *Prophecy Answered* (Westchester, IL: Good News Publishers, 1960), p. 50.

8. *The Last News* (Lee's Summit, MO: The Gospel Tract Society, Inc., n.d.), pp. 1–4.

9. John F. Walvoord, *The Revelation of Jesus Christ* (Chicago: Moody Press, 1966), p. 129. Used by permission of Moody Press.

10. Phillips, p. 105.

11. John F. Walvoord and Roy B. Zuck, *The Bible Knowledge Commentary, New Testament: New Testament Edition* (Wheaton, IL: Victor Books/Scripture Press Publications, Inc., 1983), "II Thessalonians" by Thomas L. Constable, pp. 720, 721.

12. Oliver B. Greene, *The Epistles of Paul the Apostle to the Thessalonians* (Greenville, SC: The Gospel Hour, Inc., 1964), p. 279.

13. Arthur W. Pink, *The Antichrist* (Grand Rapids: Kregel Publications, 1988), p. 41.

14. Lehman Strauss, *Daniel* (Neptune, NJ: Loizeaux Brothers, 1969), p. 342.

15. Herman A. Hoyt, *The End Times* (Chicago: Moody Press, 1969), p. 126.

16. Alva J. McClain, *Daniel's Prophecy of the Seventy Weeks,* 3d ed. (Grand Rapids: Zondervan Publishing House, 1940), p. 43.

17. William W. Orr, *A Simple Picture of the Future* (San Dimas, CA: William W. Orr Publications, n.d.), p. 16.

18. Walter K. Price, *The Coming Antichrist* (Chicago: Moody Press, 1974), p. 74.

19. Joseph Hoffman Cohn, *Will the Antichrist Be a Jew?* p. 2, quoted in Arnold Fruchtenbaum, *The Nationality of the Antichrist* (Englewood Cliffs, NJ: American Board of Missions to the Jews, Inc., n.d.), pp. 6, 7.

20. Cohn, quoted in *The Nationality of the Antichrist,* p. 22.

21. J. Dwight Pentecost, *Things to Come* (Grand Rapids: Zondervan Publishing House, 1979), p. 332.

22. Richard DeHaan, *The Antichrist and Armageddon* (Grand Rapids: Radio Bible Class, 1968), p. 6.

23. William Pettingill, *Brief Prophetic Messages*, p. 24, quoted in Arnold Fruchtenbaum, *The Nationality of the Antichrist* (Englewood Cliffs, NJ: American Board of Missions to the Jews, Inc., n.d.), pp. 23, 24.

24. S. Maxwell Coder, *The Final Chapter* (Wheaton, IL: Tyndale House Publishers, 1984), pp. 102, 103.

25. David L. Cooper. *The 70 Weeks of Daniel*, p. 57, quoted in Arnold Fruchtenbaum, *The Nationality of the Antichrist* (Englewood Cliffs, NJ: American Board of Missions to the Jews, Inc., n.d.), pp. 32, 33.

26. Cooper, quoted in *The Nationality of the Antichrist*, p. 33.

27. J. Dwight Pentecost, *Prophecy for Today* (Grand Rapids: Zondervan Publishing House, 1961), p. 84.

28. Kenneth S. Wuest, *Word Studies in the Greek New Testament,* 4 vols. (Grand Rapids: Wm. B. Eerdmans Publishing Company, 1966), vol. 3: *Prophetic Light in the Present Darkness,* p. 68.

29. M. R. DeHaan, *35 Simple Studies in the Book of Revelation* (Grand Rapids: Zondervan Publishing House, 1946), p. 184.

30. Oliver B. Greene, *Bible Prophecy* (Greenville, SC: By the Author, 1970), p. 234.

31. Price, p. 145.

32. Robert G. Gromacki, *Are These the Last Days?* (Westwood, NJ: Fleming H. Revell, 1970), pp. 117, 118.

33. Lewis, *Hidden Mysteries,* p. 110.

34. DeHaan, *The Antichrist and Armageddon,* pp. 7, 8.

35. Thomas S. McCall and Zola Levitt, *Satan in the Sanctuary* (Chicago: Moody Press, 1973), p. 92.

36. Bob Jones, III, *The Spirit of Antichrist* (Greenville, SC: Bob Jones University, 1975), p. 3.

37. Price, *The Coming Antichrist,* p. 44.

38. DeHaan, *The Antichrist and Armageddon,* pp. 7, 8.

39. Louis Goldberg, *Turbulence over the Middle East* (Neptune, NJ: Loizeaux Brothers, 1982), p. 143.

40. Hoyt, *The End Times,* p. 123.

41. Joseph M. Stowell, *Getting Ready for Antichrist* (Des Plaines, IL: Living Reality, GARBC, n.d.), pp. 26, 27.

42. Herbert C. Lockyer, "The Advent and Youth," *Cameos of Prophecy* (Grand Rapids: Zondervan Publishing House, 1942), pp. 124, 125.

43. Thomas M. Meachum, "The Judgment Seat of Christ," *Biblical Viewpoint* 11 (April 1977) : 70.

44. Jeffrey Hadden, *The Gathering Storm in the Churches* (Garden City, NY: Doubleday & Co., Inc., 1969), pp. 44, 45, 48, 51.

45. English, ed., Pilgrim Bible, p. 1662.

46. Lehman Strauss, *The Book of the Revelation* (Neptune, NJ: Loizeaux Brothers, 1964), pp. 215, 216.

47. J. Dwight Pentecost, *Things to Come,* pp. 269, 270.

48. English, ed., Pilgrim Bible, p. 1418.

49. J. Dwight Pentecost, *Will Man Survive?* (Chicago: Moody Press, 1971), pp. 162, 163.

50. Lewis Sperry Chafer, *Systematic Theology,* vol. 3 (Dallas: Dallas Seminary Press; Copyright by Author, 1948), p. 106.

51. J. Dwight Pentecost, *Will Man Survive?* p. 176.

52. "Will the Temple Be Rebuilt?" *Prophetic Witness Magazine,* August 1972, p. 159.

53. Ralph W. Neighbour and Gerald Stover, *Can the United Nations Establish World Peace?* and *Will the Jews Rebuild the Temple in Jerusalem?* (Elyria, OH: Ralph W. Neighbour, 1972), pp. 9, 10.

54. Leon J. Wood, *The Bible and Future Events* (Grand Rapids: Zondervan Publishing House, 1973), p. 136.

55. Henry Morris, *The Revelation Record* (Wheaton, IL: Tyndale House Publishers, 1983), p. 230.

56. William W. Orr, *The 1000 Year Reign of Jesus Christ!* (San Dimas, CA: William W. Orr Publications, n.d.), p. 31.

57. G. L. Murray, *Millennial Studies* (Grand Rapids: Baker Book House, 1948), p. 91.

58. J. Dwight Pentecost, *Things to Come,* p. 546.

59. Alva J. McClain, *The Greatness of the Kingdom* (Grand Rapids: Zondervan Publishing House, 1959), pp. 500–502.

60. Wood, p. 180.

61. S. Maxwell Coder, *The Final Chapter* (Wheaton, IL: Tyndale House Publishers, 1984), pp. 225, 226.

62. Carl G. Johnson, *So the Bible Is Full of Contradictions?* (Grand Rapids: New Hope Press/Baker Book House, 1983), p. 99.

63. McClain, pp. 512, 513.

64. John F. Walvoord, *The Millennial Kingdom* (Grand Rapids: Dunham, 1959), p. 328.

65. Hoyt, *The End Times,* p. 230.

66. *Vine's Expository Dictionary of New Testament Words* (Westwood, NJ: Fleming H. Revell, 1962), vol. 1, p. 268.

67. Robert L. Sumner, *Hell Is No Joke* (Grand Rapids: Zondervan Publishing House, 1959), pp. 18, 19.

68. Morris, *The Revelation Record,* p. 431.

69. George Gallup, quoted in *Hell You Say!* by Carl G. Johnson (Newtown, PA: Timothy Books, 1974), p. viii.

70. Ibid, pp. viii, ix.

71. "Modern Christians Remain Mum on Hell," *Christian Life*, August 1986, p. 15.

72. A. C. Dixon, quoted in *Hell You Say!* p. x.

73. Fred Carl Kuehner, "Heaven or Hell?" p. 24.

74. J. M. Humphrey, *The Lost Soul's First Day in Eternity* (Chicago: The Christian Witness Company, 1912), p. 29.

75. Gromacki, *Are These the Last Days?* pp. 185, 186.

76. G. Beauchamp Vick, quoted in *Hell You Say!* pp. 59, 60.

77. Catherine Dangell, quoted in *Hell You Say!* pp. 72, 73.

78. D. M. Fletcher, quoted in *Hell You Say!* pp. 74, 75.

79. Jim Mercer, quoted in *Hell You Say!* p. 118.

80. T. DeWitt Talmadge, quoted in *Hell You Say!* pp. 118, 119.

81. René Pache, *The Future Life* (Chicago: Moody Press, 1962), pp. 323, 324. Used by permission of Moody Press.

82. Emory Bancroft, *Elemental Theology,* 4th ed. (Grand Rapids: Zondervan Publishing House, 1977), p. 205.

83. James A. Borland, "Exposition of Life," in *Liberty Commentary on the New Testament,* ed. Jerry Falwell (Lynchburg, VA: Old Time Gospel Hour, 1978), p. 152.

84. J. C. Ryle, *Ryle's Expository Thoughts on the Gospels,* vol. 2 (Grand Rapids: Baker Book House, 1977), pp. 347, 348.

85. Irving S. Cobb, quoted in *Hell You Say!* p. vii.

86. Edward C. Pentecost, "Jude," *The New Testament Edition of the Bible Knowledge Commentary* (Scripture Press Publications, Inc., 1983), p. 922.

87. George H. Mundell, *The Destiny of a Lost Soul* (Fort Washington, PA: Christian Literature Crusade, 1969), pp. 7, 8. Used by permission of Christian Literature Crusade.

88. E. Johnson, "Job," *The Pulpit Commentary,* vol. 7 (Grand Rapids: Wm. B. Eerdmans Publishing Company, 1950), p. 416.

89. Harry C. Mark, *If a Man Die Shall He Live Again?* (Grand Rapids: Zondervan Publishing House, 1973), p. 106.

90. John Dick, quoted in *If a Man Die Shall He Live Again?* p. 105.

91. William E. Bierderwolf as quoted in William Striker, *What Happens after Death?* (New York: American Tract Society, 1935), p. 105. Reprinted by permission of the American Tract Society, Garland, TX.

92. Robert Gromacki, "When a Child Dies," *Confident Living,* September 1989, p. 23. Reprinted by permission from *Confident Living,* Copyright © 1989 by the Good News Broadcasting Association, Inc.

93. Dean Dan Lyons, "Human Life before Birth" (Tulsa, OK: Americans Against Abortion, n.d.), pp. 2, 3.

94. Ibid.

95. "Abortion: Where Have All the Babies Gone?" (Garland, TX: American Tract Society, n.d.), pp. 6, 7.

96. U.S., Congress, Senate, *Report of the Subcommittee on Separation of Powers,* S-158, 97th Cong., 1st sess., 1981, p. 7. Quoted in *Abortion Questions & Answers* (Cincinnati: Hayes Publishing Company, 1985), p. 40.

97. M. Matthews Roth, quoted in *Abortion Questions & Answers,* p. 41.

98. Professor H. Gordon, quoted in *Abortion Questions & Answers,* p. 41.

99. Henry M. Morris, *The Bible Has the Answer* (Grand Rapids:

Baker Book House, 1971), p. 183. Used by permission of Baker Book House.

100. C. I. Scofield, ed., Scofield Reference Bible (New York: Oxford University Press, 1909), p. 1111. See the note on Luke 23:41.

101. N. O. W., "Winning in the Game of Life," Youth for Christ Magazine, July 1946, p. 35.

102. The World Book Encyclopedia, 1985 ed., s. v. "Air," by Stanley David Gedzelman.

103 John Zoller, Heaven (New Era, MI: By the Author, 1968), p. 74.

104. Walvoord, The Revelation of Jesus Christ, p. 322.

105. Ibid.

106. Walter Scott, quoted in Carl G. Johnson, Prophecy Made Plain for Times like These (Chicago: Moody Press, 1972), p. 223.

107. Andrew Bonar, quoted in Carl G. Johnson, Prophecy Made Plain for Times like These, pp. 218, 219.

108. Robert G. Lee, Bread from Bellevue Oven, pp. 70, 71, quoted in Carl G. Johnson, Prophecy Made Plain for Times like These, pp. 226, 227. Used by permission of Sword of the Lord.

109. H. L. Willmington, The King Is Coming (Wheaton, IL: Tyndale House Publishers, 1973), p. 304.

110. Charles H. Spurgeon, Spurgeon's Sermons, vol. 1 (Grand Rapids: Zondervan Publishing House, n.d.), pp. 301, 302.

111. Tim LaHaye, Revelation Illustrated and Made Plain (Grand Rapids: Zondervan Publishing House, 1975), p. 298.

112. Herbert Lockyer, Death and the Life Hereafter (Grand Rapids: Baker Book House, 1967), p. 71. Used by permission of Baker Book House.

113 Morris, The Revelation Record, pp. 438, 439.

114. Arthur W. Pink, Exposition of the Gospel of John, vol. 1 (Swengel, PA: Bible Truth Depot, 1956), p. 351.

115. Wood, pp. 177, 178.

116. John F. Walvoord, *The Church in Prophecy* (Grand Rapids: Zondervan Publishing House, 1964), p. 174.

117. M. R. DeHaan, *Coming Events in Prophecy,* p. 9.

118. Morris, *The Revelation Record,* p. 322.

119. Warren Wiersbe, "Exposition of Hebrews Chapter 12," *The Bible Exposition Commentary,* vol. 2 (Wheaton, IL: Scripture Press, 1989), p. 326.

120. John F. Walvoord and Roy B. Zuck, *The Bible Knowledge Commentary: Old Testament Edition* (Wheaton, IL: Victor Books/ Scripture Press, 1985), *Isaiah,* by John A. Martin, p. 1067.

121. Walter Kaiser, "Isaiah's Light on the Framework for Peace," *Eternity,* December 1978, p. 24.

122. Strauss, *The Book of the Revelation,* p. 322.

123. J. Dwight Pentecost, *Things to Come,* p. 228.

124. Willmington, *The King Is Coming*, pp. 46, 47.

125. Pache, p. 252.

126. J. A. Seiss, *The Apocalypse* (Grand Rapids: Zondervan Publishing House, n.d.), p. 481.

127. Louis T. Talbot, *The Revelation of Jesus Christ* (Grand Rapids: Wm. B. Eerdmans Publishing Company, 1937), pp. 225, 226. Used by permission of Wm. B. Eerdmans Publishing Company.

128. S. Franklin Logsdon, *Is the U.S.A. in Prophecy?* (Grand Rapids: Zondervan Publishing House, 1968), pp. 25, 36.

129. Charles L. Feinberg, "The United States in Prophecy?" *Good News Broadcaster,* December 1981, p. 15. Used by permission of Lois Feinberg-Gonzenbach.

130. John F. Walvoord, *The Nations in Prophecy* (Grand Rapids: Zondervan Publishing House, 1967), pp. 174, 175.

131. Strauss, *The Book of Revelation,* p. 360.

132. Walvoord, *The Revelation of Jesus Christ,* pp. 330, 331.

133. Paul VanGorder, *Since You Asked* (Grand Rapids: Radio

Bible Class, 1980), p. 113.

134. John F. Walvoord, "Israel's Blindness," *Bibliotheca Sacra* 102 (July 1945) : 287, 288.

135. Oliver B. Greene, *Revelation* (Greenville, SC: The Gospel Hour, Inc., 1963), p. 539.

136. Charles R. Smith, "The Book of Life," *Grace Theological Journal* (June, 1985) : pp. 227, 228.

137. J. A. Seiss, *Letters to the Seven Churches* (Grand Rapids: Baker Book House, p. 1956), p. 201.

138. Walvoord, *The Revelation of Jesus Christ,* p. 82.

139. *Ibid.*

140. Warren Wiersbe, "Exposition of Revelation," *The Bible Exposition Commentary,* vol. 2, pp. 577, 578.

141. Smith, p. 223.

142. J. B. Lightfoot, *Saint Paul's Epistle to the Philippians* (Grand Rapids: Zondervan Publishing House, n.d.), p. 159.

143. Kenneth S. Wuest, *The New Testament: An Expanded Translation* (Grand Rapids: William B. Eerdmans Publishing Company, 1961), p. 160.

144. Smith, pp. 229, 230.

145. Coder, pp. 131, 132.

146. J. Dwight Pentecost, *Things to Come,* pp. 550, 551.

147. D. M. Lloyd-Jones, *Expository Sermons on II Peter* (Carlisle, PA: The Banner of Truth Trust, 1983), p. 121.

148. Walvoord, *The Revelation of Jesus Christ,* p. 143.

149. Alfred Martin, *First Corinthians* (Neptune, NJ: Loizeaux Brothers, 1989), p. 99.

150. English, ed., Pilgrim Bible, p. 18. See Genesis 10:32.

151. Henry Morris, *The Genesis Record* (Grand Rapids: Baker Book House, 1976), pp. 240–243. Used by permission of Baker Book House.

152. Thomas Radecki, M.D., NCTV Press Release, n.d.

153. Randall P. Harrison, quoted in John Langone, *Violence! Our Fastest Growing Public Health Problem* (Boston: Little, Brown and Company, 1984), p. 51.

154. C. Everett Koop, quoted in Phil Phillips and Joan Hoke, *Horror and Violence* (Lancaster, PA: Robie, Starburst Publishers, 1988), p. 99.

155. "Joy and Play Violence," *NCTV News* 4 (July–August 1983) : 12.

156. Thomas Radecki, quoted in *NCTV News* (October 1980).

157. Raymond A. Moody, *Reflections on Life after Life* (New York: Bantam Books, 1977), p. 16.

158. Robert A. Morey, *Death and the Afterlife* (Minneapolis: Bethany House Publishers, 1984), p. 264. Used by permission of Bethany House Publishers.

159. Norman Geisler, quoted in H. Wayne House and Thomas Ice, *Dominion Theology: Blessing or Curse?* (Portland, OR: Multnomah Press, 1988), back of book jacket.

160. Charles C. Ryrie, quoted in *Dominion Theology: Blessing or Curse?* back of book jacket.

161. Thomas Ice, *Dominion Theology: Blessing or Curse?* p. 16.

162. H. Wayne House, *Dominion Theology: Blessing or Curse?* pp. 17–21.

163. Greg Bahnsen, *Theonomy in Christian Ethics,* p. 39, quoted in *Dominion Theology: Blessing or Curse?* p. 115.

164. H. Wayne House and Thomas Ice, *Dominion Theology: Blessing or Curse?* p. 335.

165. Albert Barnes, "Matthew," *Barnes' Notes* (Grand Rapids: Baker Book House, 1983), p. 314.

166. Matthew Henry, "Matthew," *Matthew Henry's Commentary,* vol. 5 (New York: Fleming H. Revell, n.d.), p. 432.

167. Walvoord, *The Revelation of Jesus Christ,* p. 298.

168. William L. Pettingill, "Saints Raised at Christ's Resurrection," *Bible Questions Answered,* p. 185

169. Marvin Rosenthal, *The Pre-Wrath Rapture of the Church* (Nashville: Thomas Nelson, Inc., 1990; Copyright 1990 by Author), p. 60.

170. Ibid., p. 293.

171. Ibid., p. 172.

172. Ibid.

173. Paul S. Karleen, *The Pre-Wrath Rapture of the Church* (Langhorne, PA: B. F. Press, 1991), p. 20.

174. Renald Showers, "The Rapture of the Church," *Israel My Glory,* vol. 48, no. 2, April-May, 1990, p. 14.

175. Rosenthal, p. 185.

176. Rosenthal, p. 159.

177. Rosenthal, pp. 198, 206.

178. Rosenthal, p. 260.

179. Rosenthal, p. 35.

180. Rosenthal, pp. 295, 296.

181. Paul W. Powell, *Why Me, Lord?* (Wheaton, IL: Scripture Press, 1981), p. 113. Used by permission of Victor Books, SP Publications, Inc.

182. Phillips, *Exploring Revelation,* p. 126.

183. "Man Gives Up after 6 Tries to End It All," Orlando *Sentinal Star,* 14 January 1979.

184. Morris, *The Revelation Record,* p. 161.

185. Nina Easton, "Shirley MacLaine's Mysticism for the Masses," *The Los Angeles Times Magazine,* September 6, 1987, p. 33.

186. Benjamin Creme, *The Reappearance of the Christ and the Masters of Wisdom,* p. 110, quoted in Walter Martin, *The New Age Cult* (Minneapolis: Bethany House Publishers, 1989), p. 26. Used by permission of Bethany House Publishers.

187. Levi, *The Aquarian Gospel of Jesus the Christ,* p. 100, quoted in Walter Martin, *The New Age Cult,* p. 26.

188. Benjamin Creme, quoted in *The New Age Cult,* p. 26.

189. Foundation for Inner Peace, *A Course in Miracles,* vol. 1, p. 5, quoted in *The New Age Cult,* p. 30.

190. Foundation for Inner Peace, quoted in *The New Age Cult,* p. 28.

191. Levi, quoted in *The New Age Cult,* p. 31.

192. Jane Roberts, *Seth Speaks,* pp. 282, 283, quoted in Walter Martin, *The New Age Cult,* p. 31.

193. Foundation for Inner Peace, quoted in *The New Age Cult,* p. 31.

194. David Spangler, *Reflections on the Christ,* p. 39, quoted in Walter Martin, *The New Age Cult,* p. 32.

195. Spangler, quoted in *The New Age Cult,* p. 32.

196. Alice A. Bailey, *The Reappearance of the Christ,* pp. 116, 117, quoted in Walter Martin, *The New Age Cult,* p. 33.

197. Levi, quoted in *The New Age Cult,* p. 33.

198. Spangler, quoted in *The New Age Cult,* p. 34.

199. Walter Martin, p. 108.

200. Morris, *The Bible Has the Answer,* p. 78.

201. Scofield Reference Bible, p. 1228.

202. Ibid.

203. C. I. Scofield, ed., The New Scofield Reference Bible (New York: Oxford University Press, 1967), p. 1250.

204. John L. Benson, "Puzzled? Here's Your Answer," *Today's Living,* May/June/July 1971, p. 38.

205. J. C. Ryle, *Ryle's Expository Thoughts on the Gospels,* vol. 4, p. 112.

206. C. Samuel Storms, *Chosen for Life* (Grand Rapids: Baker Book House, 1987), p. 28. Used by permission of Baker Book House.

207. Warren W. Wiersbe, "How Rich You Are," *The Bible Exposition Commentary,* vol. 2, p. 11.

208. Edward R. Roustio, "Exposition of Ephesians 1:4," *Liberty Commentary on the New Testament,* p. 506.

209. Morris, *The Bible Has the Answer,* pp. 123, 124.

210. Arnold T. Olson, *Should I Join a Church?* (Minneapolis: F. C. Publications, n.d.), pp. 11, 12.

211. A. H. Strong, *Systematic Theology* (Valley Forge, PA: Judson Press, 1979), p. 894.

212. Kenneth H. Good, *Why Every Christian Should Be a Member of a Local Church* (Elyria, OH: Fellowship of Baptists for Home Missions, n.d.), p. 16.

213. We were unable to identify completely the source of publication for the illustration. We would appreciate any information concerning the source, and we will be pleased to include it in any subsequent edition.

214. S. Lewis Johnson, Jr., "God Gave Them Up," *Bibliotheca Sacra* 129 (April 1972) : 128.

215. Ibid., p. 132.

216. A. T. Robertson, *Word Pictures in the New Testament,* vol. 4: "The Epistles of Paul" (Grand Rapids: Baker Book House; Copyright renewal 1960 by the Sunday School Board of the Southern Baptist Convention), p. 330.

217. Arthur W. Pink, *Exposition on the Gospel of John,* p. 281.

218. J. C. Ryle, *Ryle's Expository Thoughts on the Gospels,* vol. 4, p. 156.

219. J. Vernon McGee, *Through the Bible with J. Vernon McGee,* vol. 4 (Nashville: Thomas Nelson, Inc., Publishers, 1983; Copyright 1983 by Author), p. 449.

220. Harry Ironside, *Notes on Proverbs* (New York: Loizeaux Brothers, 1967), p. 23.

221. Oliver B. Greene, *The Epistle of Paul the Apostle to the Hebrews* (Greenville, SC: The Gospel Hour, 1964), pp. 540, 541.

222. John Calvin as quoted in William R. Newell, *Hebrews Verse by Verse* (Chicago: Moody Press, 1947; Copyright 1947 by Author), p. 406.

223. John Owen, quoted in William R. Newell, *Hebrews Verse by Verse,* p. 406.

224. Newell, *Hebrews Verse by Verse,* p. 406.

225. Warren W. Wiersbe, "Hebrews," *The Bible Exposition Commentary,* vol. 2, p. 324.

226. "Now at War: 1 in Every 4 Nations," *U.S. News & World Report,* March 28, 1983, p. 11.

227. Pitrim Sorokin and Nicholas Golovin, quoted in Lehman Strauss, *God's Plan for the Future* (Grand Rapids: Zondervan Publishing House, 1965), pp. 167, 168.

228. Harry Hager, quoted in *God's Plan for the Future,* p. 170.

229. A. T. Robertson, "James," *Word Pictures in the New Testament,* vol. 6, p. 49.

230. Albert Barnes, "James," *Barnes Notes* (London: Blackie & Son, 1885; reprint ed.; ed. Robert Frew; Grand Rapids: Baker Book House, 1983), p. 66.

231. A. C. Gaebelein, *What the Bible Says about Angels* (Grand Rapids: Baker Book House, 1987), p. 101. Used by permission of Baker Book House.

232. Pentecost, *Things to Come,* p. 411.

233. S. Franklin Logsdon, *Profiles of Prophecy* (Grand Rapids: Zondervan Publishing House, 1968), p. 115.

234. James A. Stewart, *Evangelism* (Swengel, PA: Reiner Publications, 1966), pp. 88, 89.

235. Leonard Ravenhill, *America Is Too Young to Die* (Minneapolis: Bethany Fellowship, 1979; Copyright 1979 by Author), pp. 34, 35.

236. "Americans Strong on Religion but Weak in Morality— Poll," *Beckley Post–Herald,* 21 July 1984.

237. G. Christian Weiss, quoted in Carl G. Johnson, *Scriptural*

Sermon Outlines (Grand Rapids: Baker Book House, 1965), p. 64.

238 Ibid.

239. Chafer, *Systematic Theology,* vol. 7, p. 48.

240. Homer A. Kent, Jr., "Matthew," *The Wycliffe Bible Commentary* (Chicago: Moody Press, 1962), p. 950. Used by permission of Moody Press.

241. Harry Ironside, *Epistles of John* (New York: Loizeaux Brothers, 1931), p. 216.

242. Ironside, *Epistles of John*, pp. 219–221.

243. Andrei Sakharov, quoted in John Wesley White, *WWIII* (Grand Rapids: Zondervan Publishing House, 1977), p. 22.

244. Alan Munn, quoted in John Wesley White, *WWIII*, p. 22.

245. Frank Sterrett, quoted in *Last Day Messenger,* January/February 1920, p. 15.

246. Walter Spears, quoted in L. E. Maxwell, "Pessimist or Optimist," *The Prairie Overcomer,* September 1973, p. 408.

247. We were unable to find the source of publication for this poem. We would appreciate any information concerning the source, and we will be pleased to include it in any subsequent edition.

248. C. I. Scofield, "Note 4 on Justification," Scofield Reference Bible, p. 1195.

249. We were unable to find the source of publication for the poem from which these lines were taken. We would appreciate any information concerning the source, and we will be pleased to include it in any subsequent edition.

250. Charles F. Kettering, quoted in Carl G. Johnson, *Prophecy Made Plain for Times like These* (Chicago: Moody Press, 1972), p. 214.

251. Kenneth O. Gangel, "Guiding Teens Regarding Their Future," *Christian Education Monograph* (Glen Ellyn, IL: Scripture Press Ministries, 1971), p. 1.

252. Francis W. Dixon, "Our Lord's Cure for Heart Trouble," *Notes of Bible Studies Conducted by Rev. Francis W. Dixon* (Bournemouth, England: Lonsdowne Baptist Church, 1969), study no. 11.

Bibliography

Abortion Questions & Answers. Cincinnati: Hayes Publishing Company, 1985.

"Abortion: Where Have All the Babies Gone?" Garland, TX: American Tract Society, n.d.

Alnor, William M. *Soothsayers of the Second Advent.* Old Tappan, NJ: Fleming H. Revell Company, 1989.

"American War Casualties." Cincinnati: Right to Life of Greater Cincinnati, n.d.

"Americans Strong on Religion but Weak in Morality—Poll." (Beckley, WV) *Post-Herald,* 21 July 1984.

Anderson, J. Kerby. *Life, Death & Beyond.* Grand Rapids: Zondervan Publishing House, 1980.

Bancroft, Emory H. *Christian Theology.* Grand Rapids: Zondervan Publishing House, 1961.

————. *Elemental Theology.* 4th ed. Grand Rapids: Zondervan Publishing House, 1977.

Barlow, Fred. *Dead Men Tell Tales.* Mesquite, TX: Sumner Evangelistic Foundation, 1961.

Barnes, Albert. *Barnes Notes.* London: Blackie & Son, 1885; reprint ed.; ed. Robert Frew. Grand Rapids: Baker Book House, 1983.

Barnhouse, Donald G. *Exposition of Bible Doctrines.* Philadelphia: The Evangelical Foundation, 1964.

Benson, John L. "Puzzled? Here's Your Answer." *Today's Living,* May/June/July 1971.

Berry, Harold J. *Which Hell Is Eternal?* Lincoln, NE: Back to the Bible, 1969.

Blackstone W. E. *Jesus Is Coming.* Old Tappan, NJ: Fleming H. Revell Company, 1898.

Boettner, Loraine. *Immortality.* Phillipsburg, NJ: The Presbyterian and Reformed Publishing Co., 1956.

Borland, James A. "Exposition of Life." *Liberty Commentary on the New Testament.* Lynchburg, VA: Old Time Gospel Hour, 1978.

Brooks, Frederick L. *Prophetic Glimpses.* Findlay, OH: Fundamental Truth Publishers, 1939.

Brooks, Keith L. *Prophecy Answered.* Westchester, IL: Good News Publishers, 1960.

Calvin, John. *Institutes of the Christian Religion, II*, pp. 250, 251. Quoted in Carl G. Johnson, *So the Bible Is Full of Contradictions?* p. 99. Grand Rapids: New Hope Press/Baker Book House, 1983.

Chafer, Lewis Sperry. *Systematic Theology.* Dallas: Dallas Seminary Press; Copyright by Lewis Sperry Chafer, 1948.

Chilton, David. *Paradise Restored.* Tyler, TX: Reconstruction Press, 1985.

————. *The Great Tribulation.* Fort Worth: Dominion Press, 1987.

Coder, S. Maxwell. *The Final Chapter,* Wheaton, IL: Tyndale House Publishers, 1984.

Coleman, William. "The Death They Whisper About," September 23, 1977.

Comfort, Ron. *Heaven, The Perfect Place.* Murfreesboro, TN: Bill Rice Ranch, Inc., 1977.

Conroy, Helen Lacey. *Heaven Is a World.* Westchester, IL: Good News Publishers, 1970.

Constable, Thomas L. *The Bible Knowledge Commentary: New Testament Edition.* Wheaton, IL: Victor Books/Scripture Press, Inc., 1983.

Criswell, W. A. *Expository Sermons on Revelation.* Grand Rapids: Zondervan Publishing House, 1962.

DeHaan, M. R. *The Believer's Judgments.* Grand Rapids: Radio Bible Class, 1963.

————. *Coming Events in Prophecy.* Grand Rapids: Zondervan Publishing House, 1962.

――. *Heaven or Hell*. Grand Rapids: Radio Bible Class, n.d.

――. *The Judgment Seat of Christ*. Grand Rapids: Radio Bible Class, n.d.

――. *35 Simple Studies in the Book of Revelation*. Grand Rapids: Zondervan Publishing House, 1946.

DeHaan, Richard. *The Antichrist and Armageddon*. Grand Rapids: Radio Bible Class, 1968.

――. "Bible Questions Answered." Source not recorded.

――. *Studies in Second Peter*. Wheaton, IL: Scripture Press, 1977.

Dixon, Francis W. *Notes of Bible Studies Conducted by Rev. Francis W. Dixon*. Bournemouth, England: Lonsdowne Baptist Church, 1969.

Easton, Nina. "Shirley MacLain's Mysticism for the Masses." *The Lost Angeles Times Magazine,* September 6, 1987.

English, E. Schuyler, ed. Pilgrim Bible. New York: Oxford University Press, Inc., 1948.

Epp, Theodore. *Practical Studies in Revelation*. 2 vols. Lincoln, NE: Back to the Bible, 1969.

Feinberg, Charles L. "The United States in Prophecy?" *Good News Broadcaster,* December 1981, pp. 12–15.

Fruchtenbaum, Arnold. *The Nationality of the Antichrist*. Englewood Cliffs, NJ: American Board of Missions to the Jews, Inc., n.d.

Gaebelein, A. C. *What the Bible Says about Angels*. Grand Rapids: Baker Book House, 1987.

Gangel, Kenneth O. "Guiding Teens Regarding Their Future." *Christian Education Monograph*. Glen Ellyn, IL: Scripture Press Ministries, 1971.

Goldberg, Louis. *Turbulence over the Middle East*. Neptune, NJ: Loizeaux Brothers, 1982.

Good, Kenneth H. "Why Every Christian Should Be a Member of a Local Church." Elyria, OH: Fellowship of Baptists for Home Missions, n.d.

Greene, Oliver B. *Bible Prophecy.* Greenville, SC: By the Author, 1970.

———. *The Epistle of Paul the Apostle to the Hebrews.* Greenville, SC: The Gospel Hour, Inc., 1964.

———. *The Epistle of Paul the Apostle to the Thessalonians.* Greenville, SC: The Gospel Hour, 1964.

———. *Heaven and Other Sermons.* Greenville, SC: The Gospel Hour, Inc., 1969.

———. *Revelation.* Greenville, SC: The Gospel Hour, Inc. 1963.

Gromacki, Robert. *Are These the Last Days?* Westwood, NJ: Fleming H. Revell, 1970.

———. "When a Child Dies." *Confident Living,* September 1989.

Hadden, Jeffrey. *The Gathering Storm in the Churches.* Garden City, NJ: Doubleday & Company, 1969.

Henry, Matthew. "Matthew." *Matthew Henry's Commentary,* Vol. 5. New York: Fleming H. Revell, n.d.

Hough, Robert Ervin. *The Christian after Death.* Chicago: Moody Press, 1947.

House, H. Wayne, and Ice, Thomas. *Dominion Theology: Blessing or Curse?* Portland: Multnomah Press, 1988.

Hoyt, Herman A. *The End Times.* Chicago: Moody Press, 1969.

Humphrey, J. M. *The Lost Soul's First Day in Eternity,* p. 29. Quoted in Carl G. Johnson, *Hell You Say!* pp. 47, 48. Newtown, PA: Timothy Books, 1974.

Ironside, Harry A. *Epistles of John.* Neptune, NJ: Loizeaux Brothers, 1931.

———. *Notes on the Book of Proverbs.* Neptune, NJ: Loizeaux Brothers, 1967.

Johnson, Carl G. *The Account Which We Must Give.* Schaumburg, IL: Regular Baptist Press, 1990.

———. *Hell You Say!* Newtown, PA: Timothy Books, 1974.

———. *Prophecy Made Plain for Times like These.* Chicago: Moody Press, 1972.

————. *Ready for Anything.* Minneapolis: Bethany Fellowship, 1968.

————. *Scriptural Sermon Outlines.* Grand Rapids: Baker Book House, 1965.

————. *So the Bible Is Full of Contradictions?* Grand Rapids: New Hope Press, 1983.

Johnson, E. "Job." *The Pulpit Commentary,* Vol. 7. Grand Rapids: Wm. B. Eerdmans Publishing Company, 1950.

Johnson, S. Lewis, Jr. "God Gave Them Up." *Bibliotheca Sacra* 129. (April 1972) : 124–133.

Jones, Bob III. *The Spirit of Antichrist.* Greenville, SC: Bob Jones University, 1975.

"Joy and Play Violence." *NCTV News,* July–August 1983, p. 12.

Kaiser, Walter. "Isaiah's Light on the Framework for Peace." *Eternity,* December 1978.

Karleen, Paul S. *The Pre-Wrath Rapture of the Church: Is it Biblical?* Langhorne, PA: BF Press, 1991.

Kennedy, D. James. *America at the Brink.* Fort Lauderdale: Coral Ridge Ministries, n.d.

Kent, Homer A., Jr. "Matthew." *The Wycliffe Bible Commentary.* Chicago: Moody Press, 1962.

Kuehner, Fred Carl. "Heaven or Hell?" *Christianity Today.* Date and page number not recorded.

LaHaye, Tim. *Revelation Illustrated and Made Plain,* Rev. Ed. Grand Rapids: Zondervan Publishing House, 1975.

Langone, John. *Violence! Our Fastest Growing Public Health Problem.* Boston: Little, Brown and Company, 1984.

Larkin, Clarence. *The Book of Revelation.* Philadelphia: Clarence Larkin Estate, 1919.

The Last News. Lee's Summit, MO: The Gospel Tract Society, Inc., n.d.

Lee, Robert G. *Bread from Bellevue Oven.* Murfreesboro, TN: Sword of the Lord, 1947.

Lewis, W. Myrddin. *Hidden Mysteries.* Unknown: By the Author, 1965.

Lightfoot, J. B. *Saint Paul's Epistle to the Philippians.* Grand Rapids: Zondervan Publishing House, n.d.

Linton, John. *Tears in Heaven and Other Sermons.* Philadelphia: Westbrook, 1942.

Little, Robert J. *Here's Your Answer.* Chicago: Moody Press, 1967.

Lloyd-Jones, D. M. *Expository Sermons on II Peter.* Carlisle, PA: The Banner of Truth Trust, 1983.

Lockyer, Herbert C. *Cameos of Prophecy.* Grand Rapids: Zondervan Publishing House, 1942.

————. *Death and the Life Hereafter.* Grand Rapids: Baker Book House, 1967.

Logsdon, S. Franklin. *Is the U. S. A. in Prophecy?* Grand Rapids: Zondervan Publishing House, 1968.

————. *Profiles of Prophecy.* Grand Rapids: Zondervan Publishing House, 1964.

Lyons, Dean Dan, "Human Life before Birth." *Life.* Date and page number not recorded.

Macpherson, Ian. *News of the World to Come.* Eastbourne, Sussex, England: Prophetic Witness Publishing House, 1973.

"Man Gives Up after 6 Tries to End It All." (Orlando) *Sentinel Star,* 14 January 1979.

Mark, Harry C. *If a Man Die Shall He Live Again?* Grand Rapids: Zondervan Publishing House, 1973.

Martin, Alfred. *First Corinthians.* Neptune, NJ: Loizeaux Brothers, 1989.

Martin, John. "Isaiah," *The Bible Knowledge Commentary: Old Testament Edition.* ed. John F. Walvoord and Roy B. Zuck. Wheaton: Victor Books/Scripture Press, 1985.

Martin, Walter. *The New Age Cult.* Minneapolis: Bethany House Publishers, 1989.

Maxwell, L. E. "Pessimist or Optimist." *The Prairie Overcomer,* September 1973.

McCall, Thomas, and Levett, Zola. *Satan in the Sanctuary.* Chicago: Moody Press, 1973.

McClain, Alva J. *Daniel's Prophecy of the Seventy Weeks.* 3d ed. Grand Rapids: Zondervan Publishing House, 1940.

———. *The Greatness of the Kingdom.* Grand Rapids: Zondervan Publishing House, 1959.

McDowell, Josh, and Don Stewart. *Answers to Tough Questions.* San Bernardino, CA: Here's Life Publishers, 1980.

McGee, J. Vernon. *Through the Bible with J. Vernon McGee,* Vol. 4. Nashville: Thomas Nelson, Inc., 1983. Copyright 1983 by Author.

Meachum, Thomas M. "The Judgment Seat of Christ." *Biblical Viewpoint* 11 (April 1977).

"Modern Christians Remain Mum on Hell." *Christian Life.* August 1986, p. 15.

Moody, Dwight L. *Heaven.* Chicago: Moody Press, n.d.

Moody, Raymond A. *Reflections on Life after Life.* New York: Bantam Books, 1977.

Morey, Robert A. *Death and the Afterlife.* Minneapolis: Bethany House Publishers, 1984.

Morris, Henry M. *The Bible Has the Answer.* Grand Rapids: Baker Book House, 1971.

———. *The Genesis Record.* Grand Rapids: Baker Book House, 1976.

———. *The Revelation Record.* Wheaton, IL: Tyndale House Publishers, 1983.

Mundell, George H. *The Destiny of a Lost Soul.* Fort Washington, PA: Christian Literature Crusade, 1969.

Munsey, William Elbert. *Eternal Retribution.* Murfreesboro, TN: Sword of the Lord Publishers, 1951.

Murray, B. L. *Millennial Studies.* Grand Rapids: Baker Book House, 1948.

Neighbour, Ralph W., Sr., and Stover, Gerald. *Can the United Nations*

Establish World Peace? and *Will the Jews Rebuild the Temple in Jerusalem?* Elyria, OH: Ralph W. Neighbour, 1972.

Newell, William R. *The Book of the Revelation.* Chicago: Moody Press, 1935.

————. *Hebrews Verse by Verse.* Chicago: Moody Press, 1947. Copyright 1947 by Author.

North, Brownlow. *The Rich Man and Lazarus.* Carlisle, PA: Banner of Truth Trust, 1961.

"Now at War: 1 in Every 4 Nations." *U.S. News & World Report,* March 28, 1983.

N.O.W. "Winning the Game of Life." *Youth for Christ Magazine,* July 1946.

Olson, Arnold T. "Should I Join a Church?" Minneapolis: F. C. Publications, n.d.

Orr, William W. *The 1000 Year Reign of Jesus Christ!* San Dimas, CA: William W. Orr Publications, n.d.

————. *The Rise and Fall of the United States.* San Dimas, CA: William W. Orr Publications, n.d.

————. *A Simple Picture of the Future.* San Dimas, CA: William W. Orr Publications, n.d.

Ostling, Richard N. "Time for a New Temple?" *Time,* October 16, 1989.

Pache, René. *The Future Life.* Chicago: Moody Press, 1962.

Paton, John I. *Bible Questions Answered.* Lincoln, NE: Back to the Bible, 1969.

Pentecost, J. Dwight. *Prophecy for Today.* Grand Rapids: Zondervan Publishing House, 1961.

————. *Things to Come.* Grand Rapids: Zondervan Publishing House, 1979.

————. *Will Man Survive?* Chicago: Moody Press, 1971.

Pentecost, Edward C. "Jude." *The New Testament Edition of the Bible Knowledge Commentary.* Wheaton, IL: Scripture Press, 1983.

Pettingill, William L. *Bible Questions Answered.* Grand Rapids: Zondervan Publishing House, 1979.

Phillips, John. *Exploring the Future*. Nashville: Thomas Nelson, Inc., Publishers, 1983.

————. *Exploring Revelation*. Chicago: Moody Press, 1987.

Phillips, Phil, and Hake, Joan. *Horror and Violence*. Lancaster, PA: Starburst, Inc., 1988.

Pickering, Hy. *Heaven the Home of the Redeemed*. London: Pickering & Inglis, n.d.

Pink, Arthur W. *The Antichrist*. Grand Rapids: Kregel Publications, 1988.

————. *Exposition of the Gospel of John,* Vol. 1. Swengel, PA: Bible Truth Depot, 1956.

Powell, Paul W. *Why Me, Lord?* Wheaton, IL: Scripture Press, 1981.

Price, Walter K. *The Coming Antichrist*. Chicago: Moody Press, 1974.

Ravenhill, Leonard. *America Is Too Young to Die*. Minneapolis: Bethany Fellowship, Inc., 1979. Copyright 1979 by Author.

Rice, John R. *Bible Facts about Heaven*. Murfreesboro, TN: Sword of the Lord Publishers, 1940.

Roberts, Jane. *Seth Speaks*. Quoted in Walter Martin, *The New Age Cult*. Minneapolis: Bethany House Publishers, 1989.

Robertson, A. T. *Word Pictures in the New Testament*. Vol. 4: *The Epistles of Paul;* and Vol. 6: *The General Epistles and the Revelation of John*. Grand Rapids: Baker Book House, 1933. Renewal 1960 by the Sunday School Board of the Southern Baptist Convention.

Rosenthal, Marvin. *The Pre-Wrath Rapture of the Church*. Nashville: Thomas Nelson Publishers, 1990.

Roustio, Edward R. "Exposition of Ephesians 1:4." *Liberty Commentary on the New Testament*. Lynchburg, VA: Old Time Gospel Hour, 1978.

Ryle, J. C. *Ryle's Expository Thoughts on the Gospels,* Vol. 2. Grand Rapids: Baker Book House, 1977.

————. *Ryle's Expository Thoughts on the Gospels,* Vol. 4. Grand Rapids: Baker Book House, 1977.

Sale-Harrison, L. *The Judgment Seat of Christ.* New York: Sale-Harrison Publications, 1938.

Scofield, C. I. New Scofield Reference Bible. New York: Oxford University Press, 1967.

————. Scofield Reference Bible. New York: Oxford University Press, 1909.

Scott, Walter. *Exposition of the Revelation of Jesus Christ.* London: Pickering & Inglis, n.d.

Scroggie, W. Graham. *What About Heaven?* Fort Washington, PA: Christian Literature Crusade, 1940.

Seiss, J. A. *The Apocalypse.* Grand Rapids: Zondervan Publishing House, n.d.

————. *Letters to the Seven Churches.* Grand Rapids: Baker Book House, 1956.

Sheler, Jeffery L. "A Revelation in the Middle East." *U.S. News & World Report,* November 19, 1990, pp. 67, 68.

Showers, Renald. "The Rapture of the Church." *Israel My Glory,* Vol. 48, No. 2, April-May, 1990, p. 14.

Smith, Charles R. "The Book of Life." *Grace Theological Journal* 6 (Fall 1985) : 219–230.

Smith, J. B. *A Revelation of Jesus Christ.* Scottdale, PA: Mennonite Publishing House, 1961.

Smith, Wilbur M. *The Biblical Doctrine of Heaven.* Chicago: Moody Press, 1968.

————. *World Crises and the Prophetic Scriptures.* Chicago: Moody Press, 1950.

Spurgeon, Charles H. *Spurgeon's Sermons,* Vol. 1. Grand Rapids: Zondervan Publishing House, Publishing House, n.d.

Stewart, James A. *Evangelism.* Swengel, PA: Reiner Publications, 1966.

Storms, C. Samuel. *Chosen for Life.* Grand Rapids: Baker Book House, 1987.

Stowell, Joseph II. *Getting Ready for Antichrist.* Des Plaines, IL: Living Reality, GARBC, n.d.

Strauss, Lehman. *The Book of the Revelation.* Neptune, NJ: Loizeaux Brothers, 1964.

———. *Daniel.* Neptune, NJ: Loizeaux Brothers, 1969.

———. *God's Plan for the Future.* Grand Rapids: Zondervan Publishing House, 1965.

Striker, William. *What Happens after Death?* New York: American Tract Society, 1935.

Strong, A. H. *Systematic Theology.* Valley Forge, PA: Judson Press, 1979.

Sumner, Robert L. *Hell Is No Joke.* Grand Rapids: Zondervan Publishing House, 1959.

Summers, Ray. *The Life Beyond.* Nashville, TN: Broadman Press, 1959.

Talbot, Louis T. *The Revelation of Jesus Christ.* Grand Rapids: Wm. B. Eerdmans Publishing Company, 1937.

Torrey, R. A. *Practical and Perplexing Questions Answered.* Chicago: Moody Press, 1908.

VanGorder, Paul R. *Since You Asked.* Grand Rapids: Radio Bible Class, 1980.

Vine, W. E. *Vine's Expository Dictionary of New Testament Words.* Westwood, NJ: Fleming H. Revell, 1962.

Wallis, Reginald. *The New Home.* New York: Loizeaux Brothers, n.d.

Walvoord, John F. *The Church in Prophecy.* Grand Rapids: Zondervan Publishing House, 1964.

———. *Daniel.* Chicago: Moody Press, 1971.

———. "Israel's Blindness." *Bibliotheca Sacra* 102 (July 1945) : 280–290.

———. *The Millennial Kingdom.* Grand Rapids: Dunham, 1959.

————. *The Nations in Prophecy.* Grand Rapids: Zondervan Publishing House, 1967.

————. *The Prophecy Knowledge Handbook.* Wheaton, IL: Scripture Press, 1990.

————. *The Revelation of Jesus Christ.* Chicago: Moody Press, 1966.

Walvoord, John F., and Zuck, Roy B. *The Bible Knowledge Commentary: New Testament Edition.* Wheaton, IL: Victor Books/Scripture Press, 1983.

————. *The Bible Knowledge Commentary: Old Testament Edition.* Wheaton, IL: Victor Books/Scripture Press, 1985.

Weaver, Jonathan. *Heaven.* Dayton, OH: U. B. Publishing House, 1899.

What Happens after Death? New York: Funk & Wagnalls Company, 1916.

White, John Wesley. *WWIII.* Grand Rapids: Zondervan Publishing House, 1977.

Wiersbe, Warren W. *The Bible Exposition Commentary,* 2 Vols. Wheaton, IL: Scripture Press, 1989.

————. "Exposition of Revelation." *The Bible Exposition Commentary,* 2 Vols. Wheaton, IL: Scripture Press, 1989.

————. "How Rich You Are." *The Bible Exposition Commentary,* 2 Vols. Wheaton, IL: Scripture Press, 1989.

Willke, J. C. , and Mrs. J. C. *Abortion Questions & Answers.* Cincinnati: Hayes Publishing Company, 1985.

"Will the Temple Be Rebuilt?" *Prophetic Witness Magazine,* August 1972.

Willmington, Harold L. *The King Is Coming.* Wheaton, IL: Tyndale House Publishers, 1973.

Wood, Leon J. *The Bible and Future Events.* Grand Rapids: Zondervan Publishing House, 1973.

World Book Encyclopedia, 1985 ed., S. v. "Air," by Stanley David Gedzelman.

Wuest, Kenneth S. *Word Studies in the Greek New Testament.* 4 vols. Grand Rapids: Wm. B. Eerdmans Publishing Company, 1966. Vol. 3: *Prophetic Light in the Present Darkness.*

———. *The New Testament: An Expanded Translation.* Grand Rapids: Wm. B. Eerdmans Publishing Company, 1961.

Zoller, John. *Heaven.* New Era, MI: By the Author, 1968.

Scripture Index

General Index